ALL DOGS ARE BEAUTIFUL
-BOOK II-

A CURATED COLLECTION OF INTERNATIONAL DOG PHOTOGRAPHY

CAROL GRAHAM

THIS BOOK IS DEDICATED TO ALL DOGS, DOG OWNERS AND RESCUES & SHELTERS AROUND THE WORLD.

Our dogs bring us endless love and devotion. Without the ongoing help of rescues and no kill shelters helping to save and care for the unwanted or abandoned our world would be a much darker place.

This is a curated collection of international photographers.

Special Thanks to Our Great Group of International Photographers:
DRZ, Alondra Pavon, Alvan Nee, Clarke Sanders, Connor Home, Flouffy, Herbert Goetsch, Jamie Street, SI Janko Ferlic, Jay Wennington, Joe Hepburn, Josephy Reckziegel, Josh Hild, Julio Bernal, Karsten Winegeart, Kendall Pena, Kerwin Elias, Kieran White, Kinshuk Bose, Massimo Negrell, Michael G, Mladen Scekic, Nail Gilfanov, Natalia Kvitovska, Nick Fewings, Nicholas Falgetelli, Omar Flores, Oscar Sutton, Philippe Nick, Ralu Gal, Roberto Nickson, Ryan Klaus, Seye Kuyinu, Stephen Goldberg, Steph Wilson, Tadeusz Lakota, Tamara Bellis, Taylor Kopel, Ton Nettos, T-R Photography, Wannes de Mol.

Karsten Winegeart (Cover Image).

In addition to honoring all dogs, large and small, plus rescues and shelters worldwide, we are happy to promote the works of the photographers in this book. Some are professional, some amateur and some are hobbyists. Whatever their actual classification the dog photos in this book are extraordinary and catch the spirit of these wonderful animals.

Many photographers in this book are available for hire. More of their photo works on additional subjects can be found at www.Unsplash.com (a Division of Getty Images). Their contact information can be found on their individual Unsplash pages or contact us and we will be happy to help you connect with them for your next project.

If interested or if you have your own quality pet images you'd like to share for the next book please feel free to contact photobookpublishers@gmail.com.

We're excited!
Future books coming out soon for highlighting localized pets and pet owners with a portion of the proceeds to go toward a chosen rescue or shelter in that local area. For more information on this please feel free to send us an email!

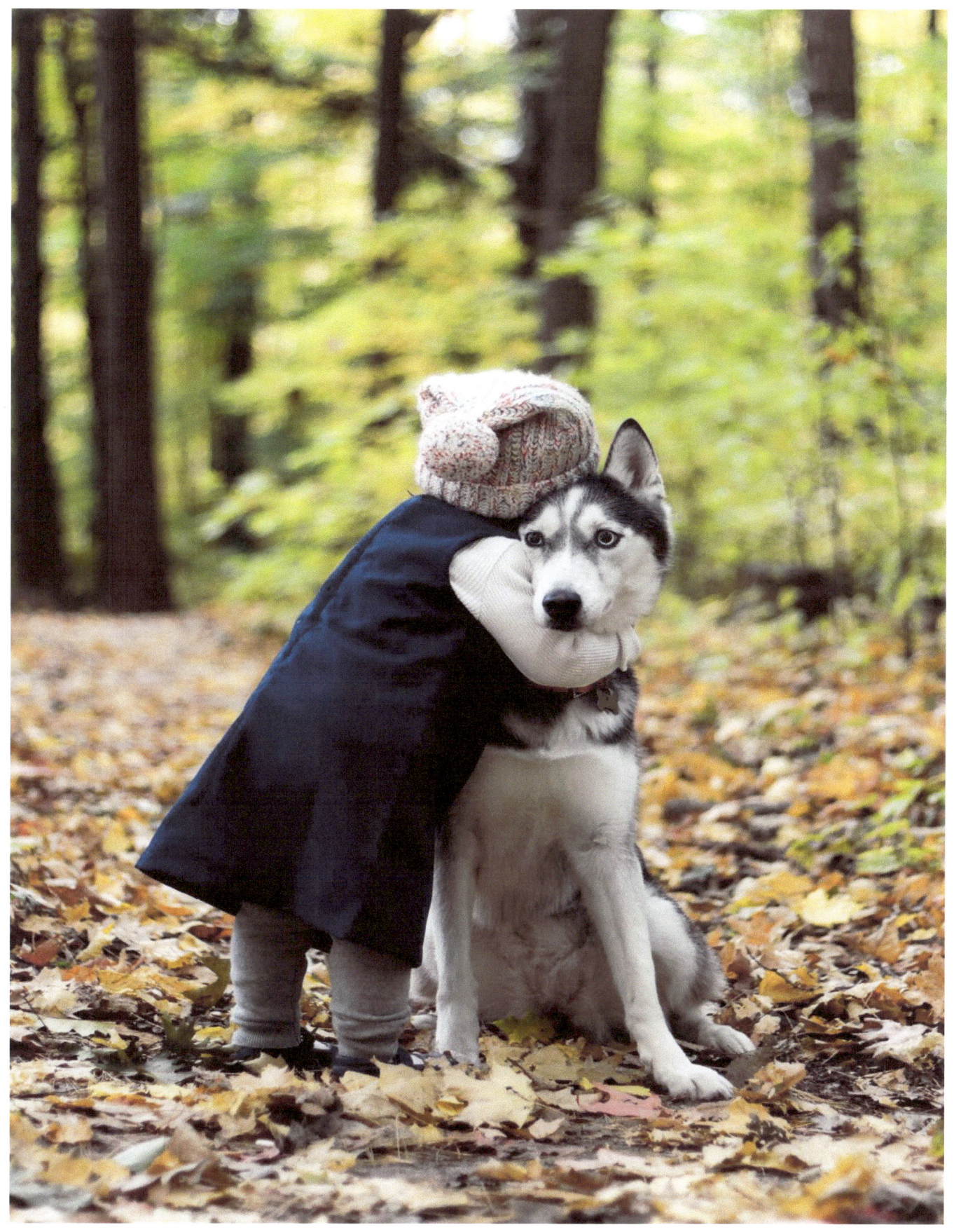

Photographer: DRZ

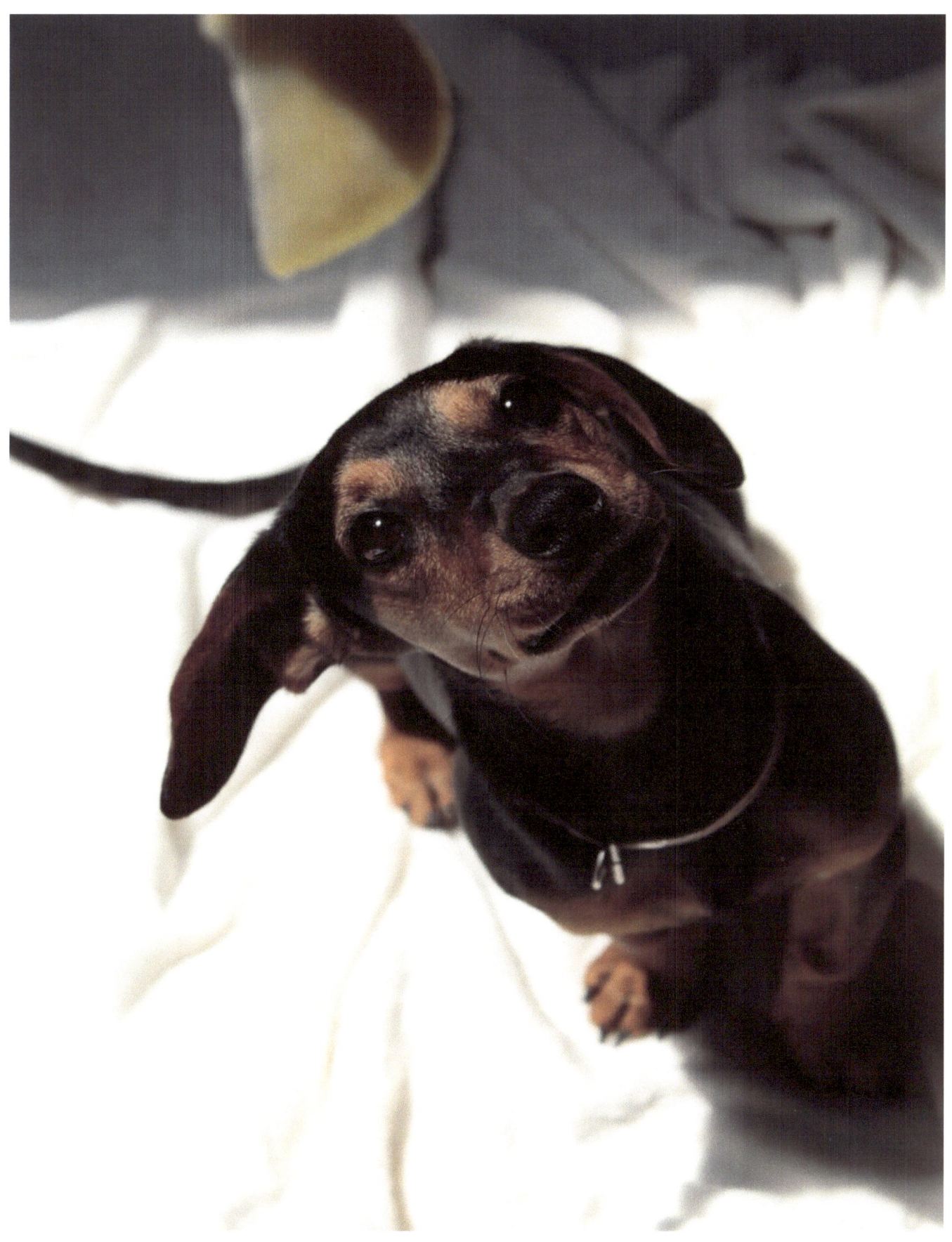

Photographer: Alondra Pavon

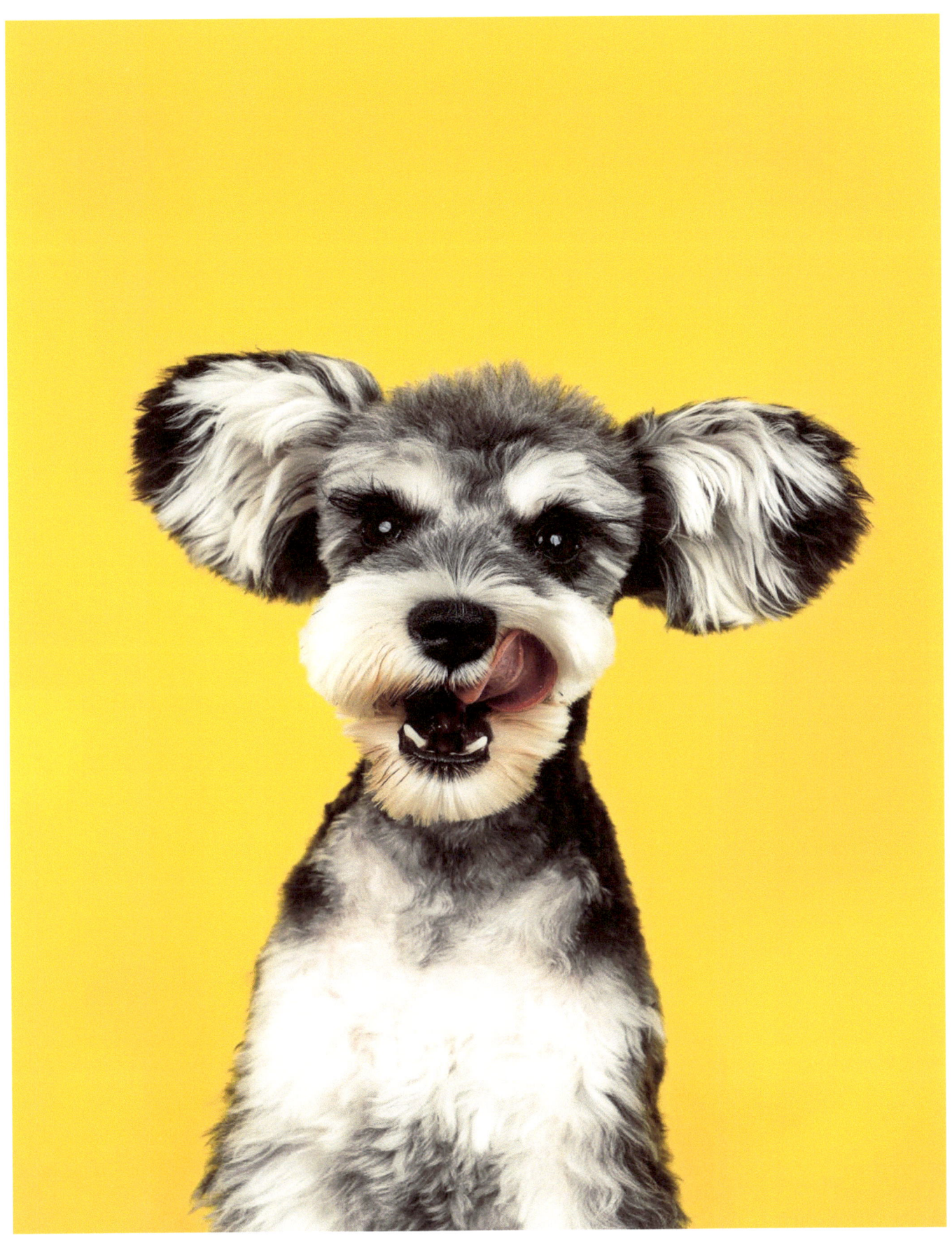

Photographer: Alvan Nee – Shanghai, China

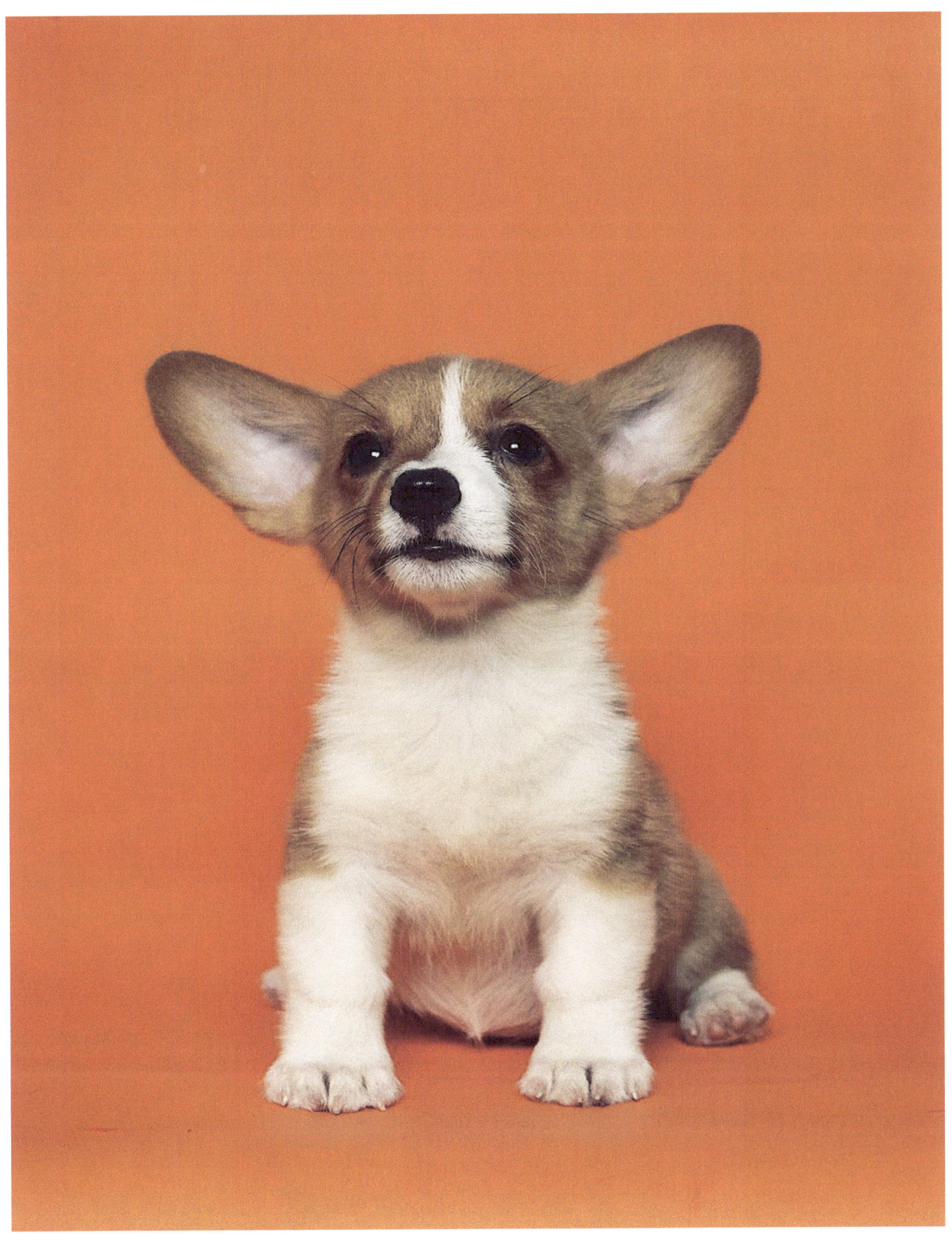

Photographer: Clarke Sanders – Minneapolis, Minnesota

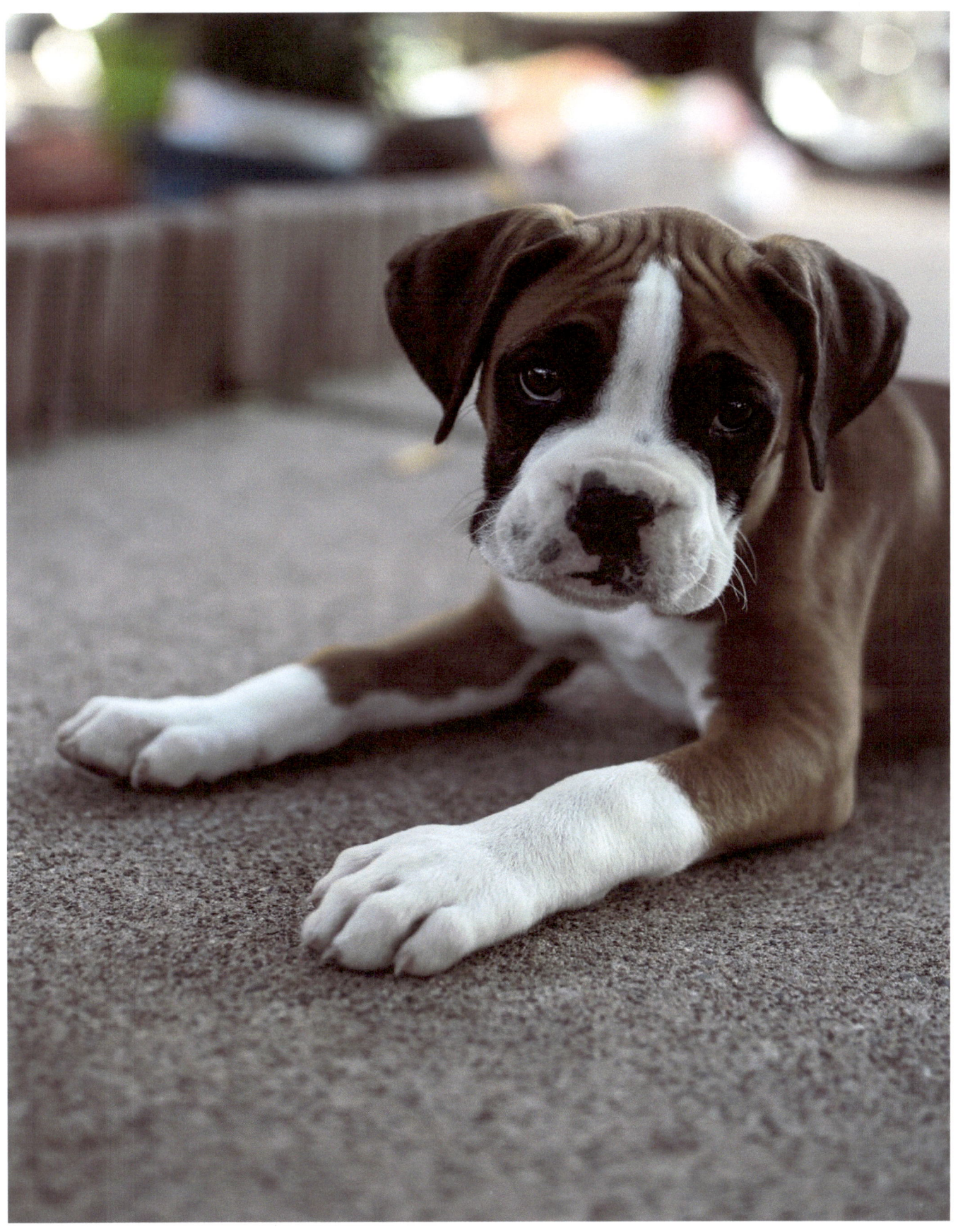

Photographer: Connor Home

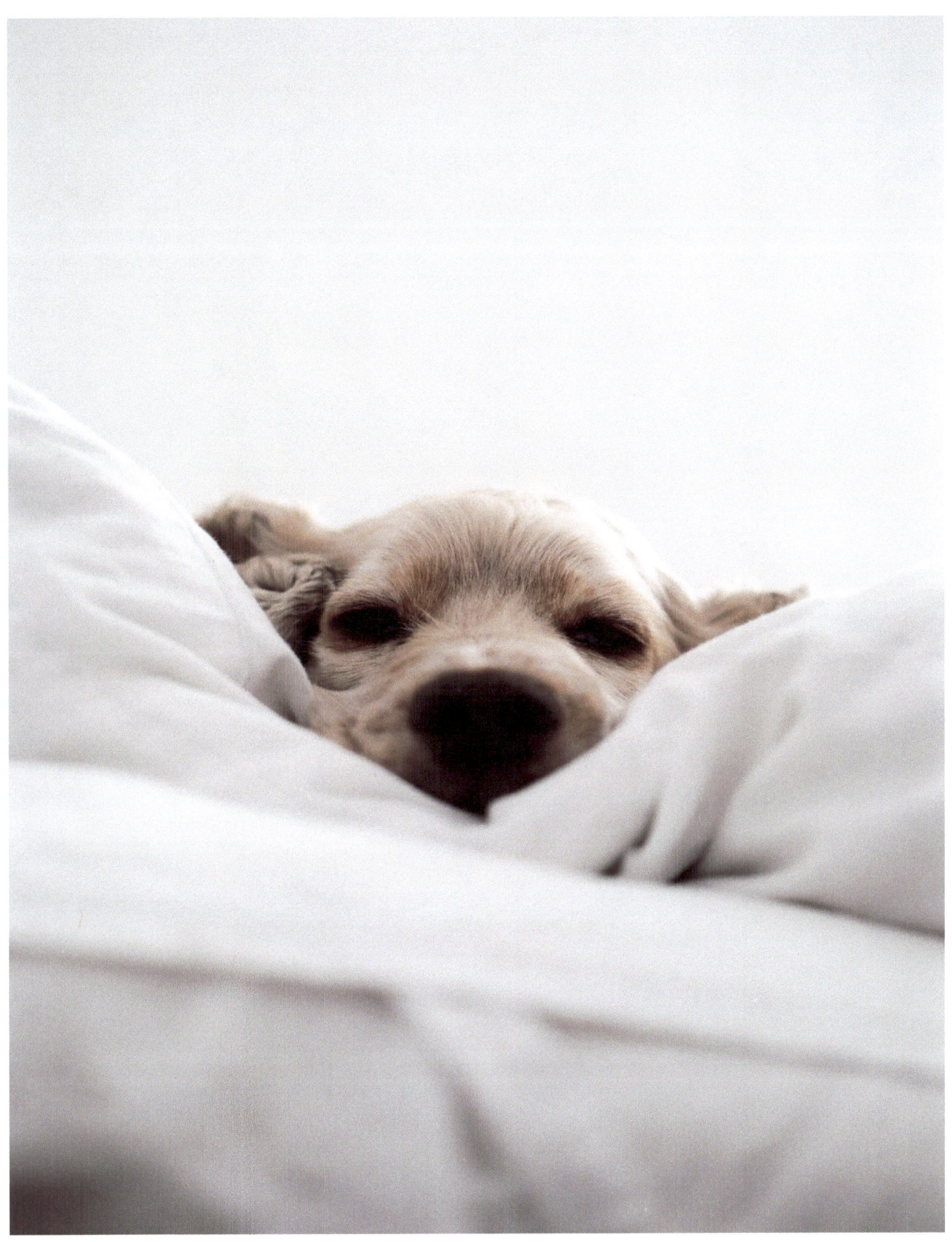

Photographer: Connor Home

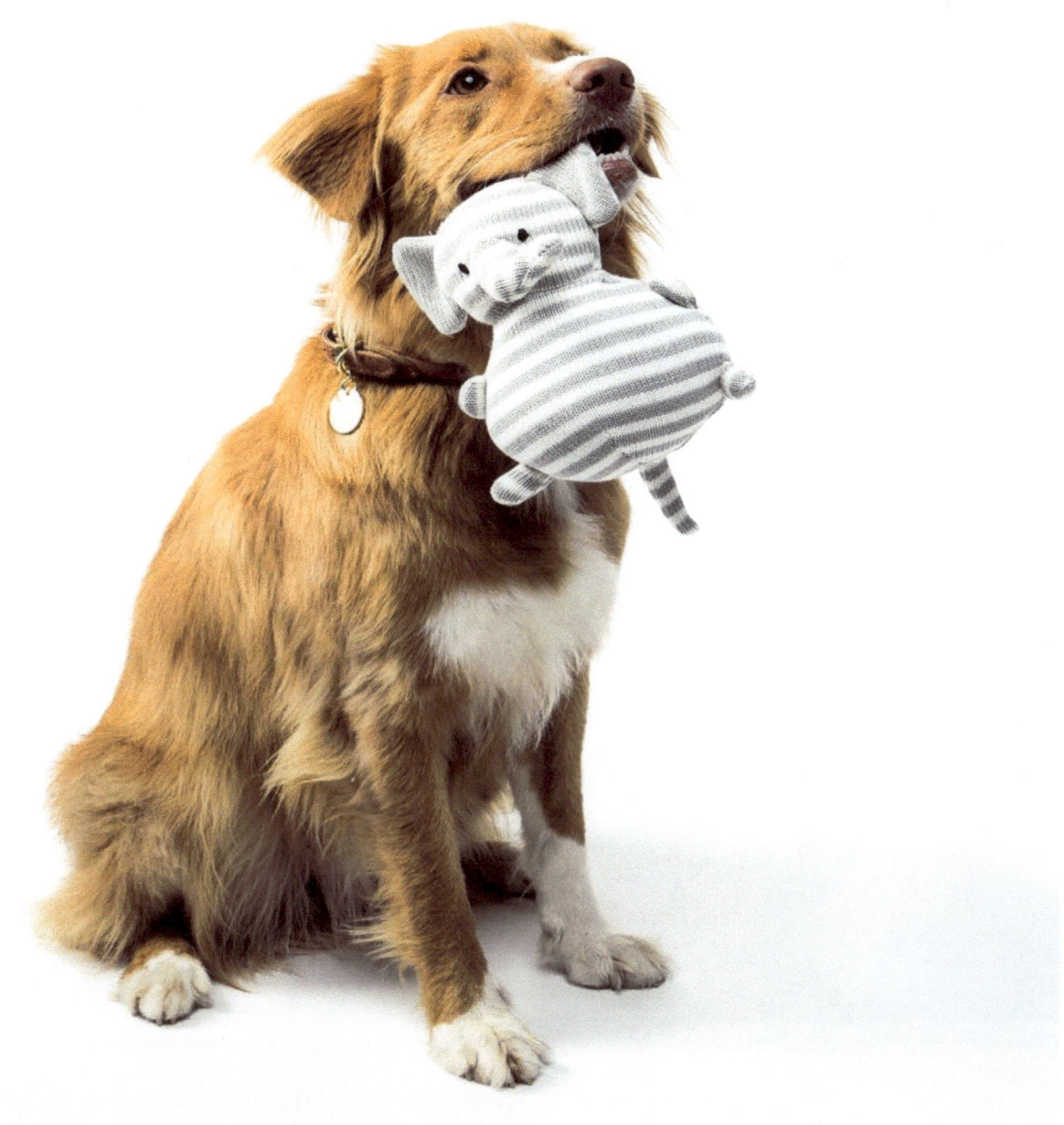

Photographer: Flouffy

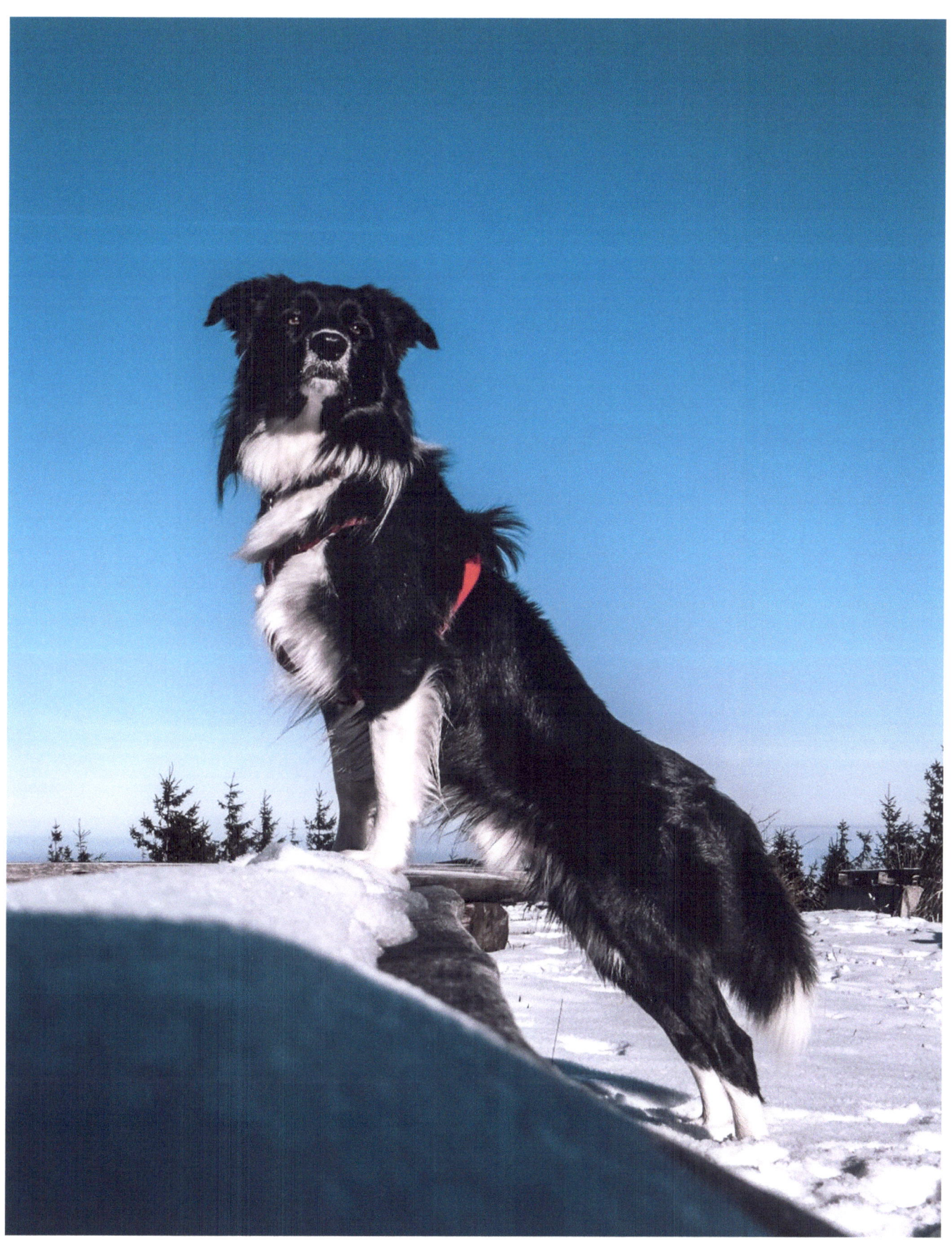

Photographer: Tadeusz Lakota – Czech Republic

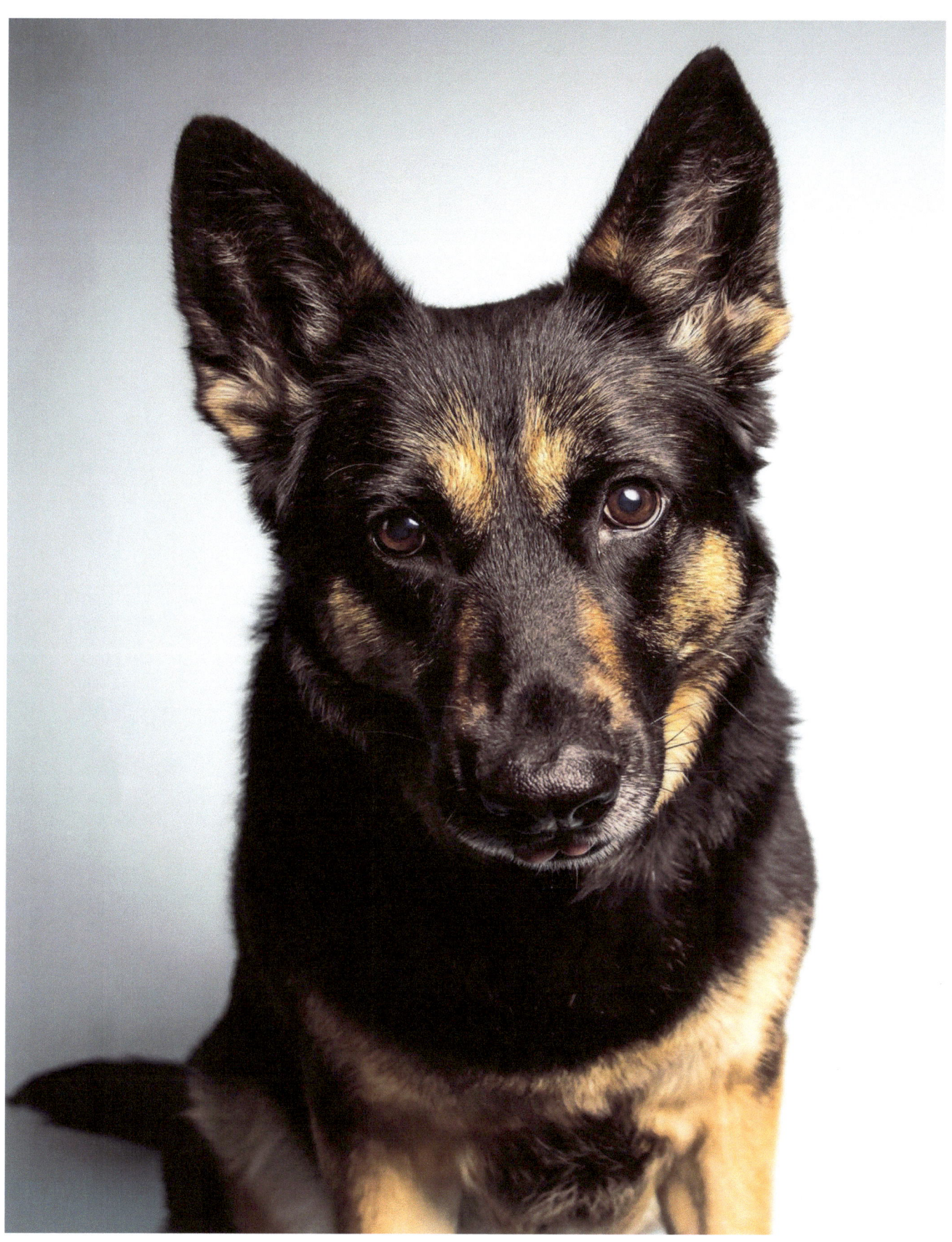

Photographer: Micheal G – New Mexico (Rescue Photographer)

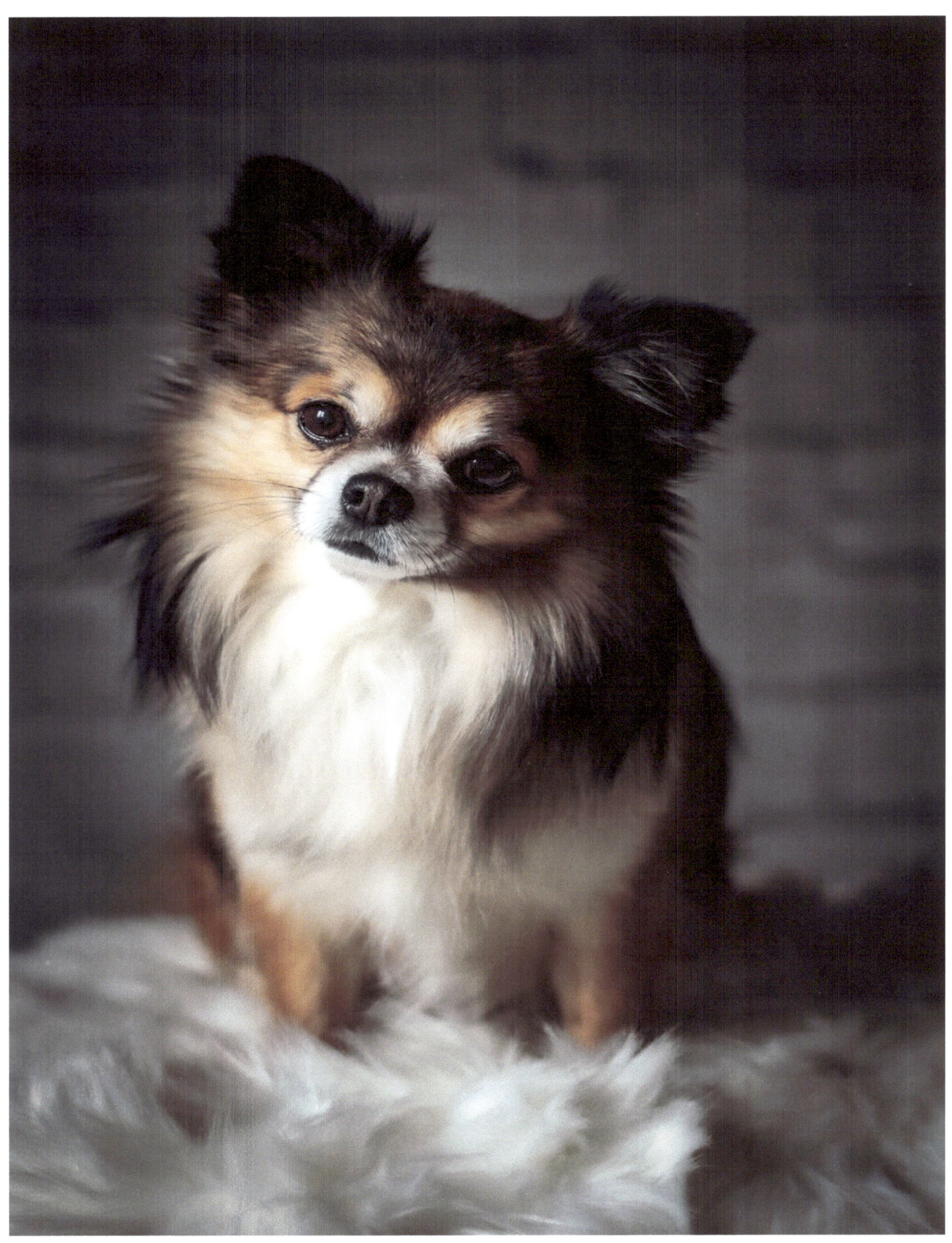

Photographer: Herbert Goetsch – Meran, Italy

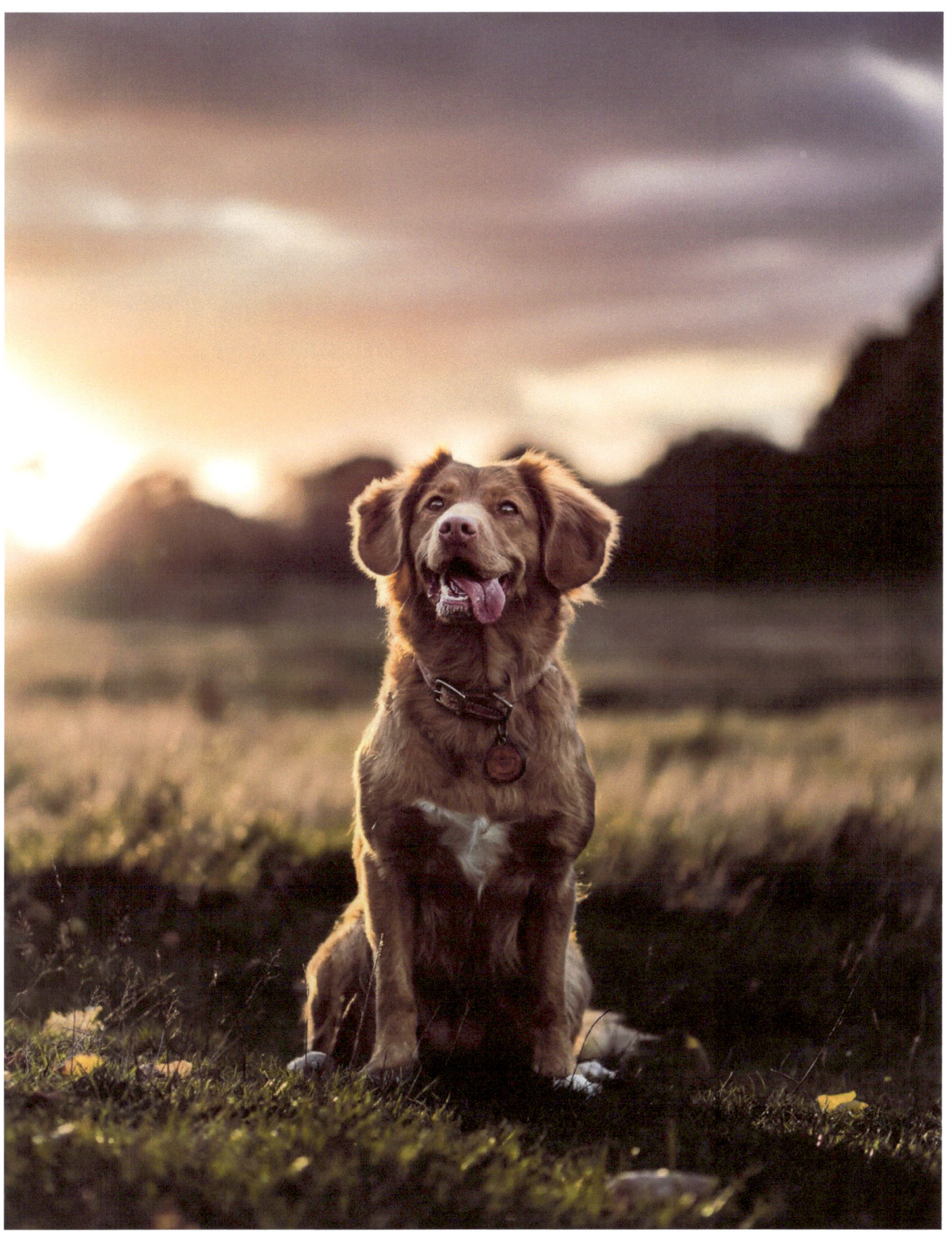

Photographer: Jamie Street – Surrey, UK

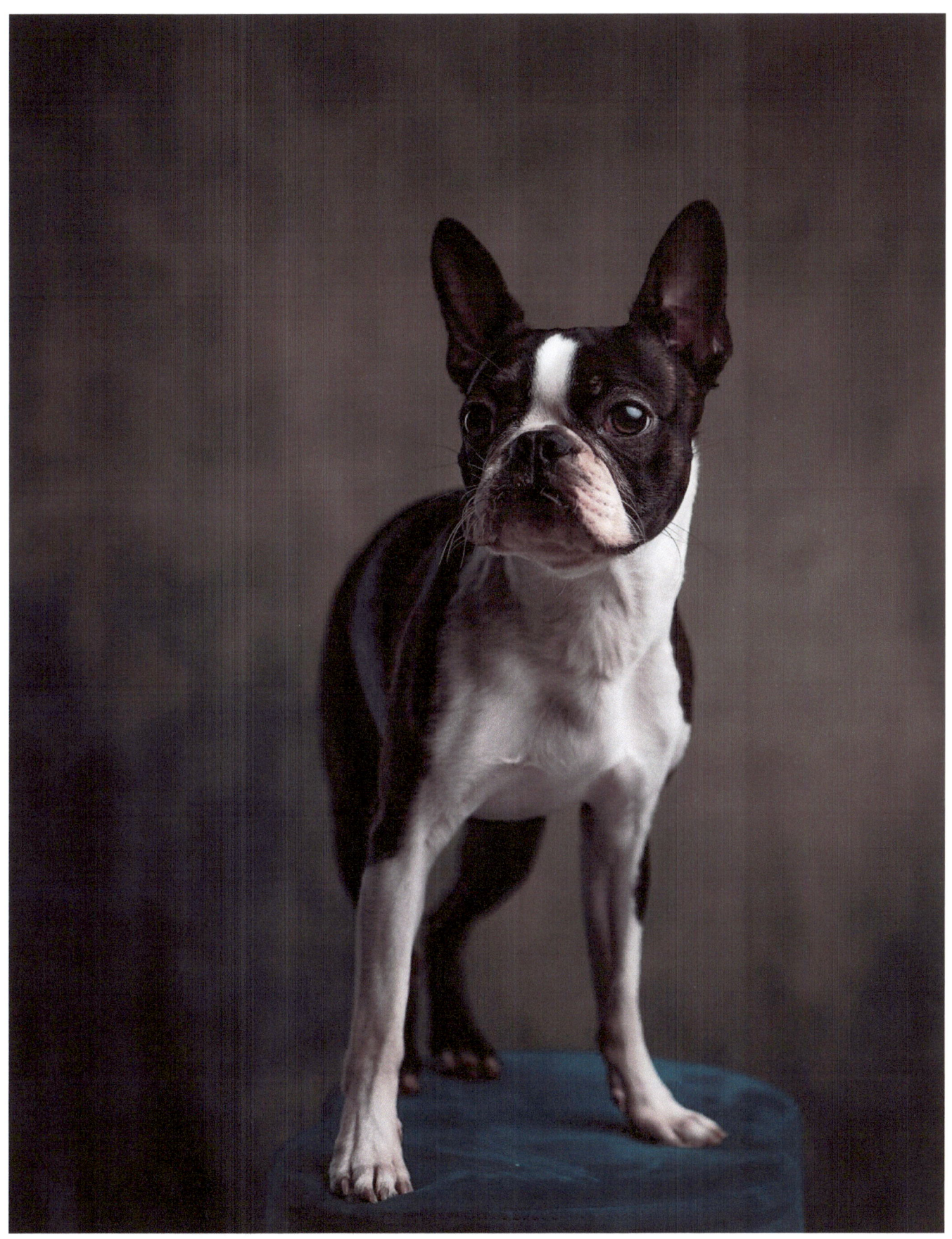

Photographer: SI Janko Ferlic – Visakfors, Sweden

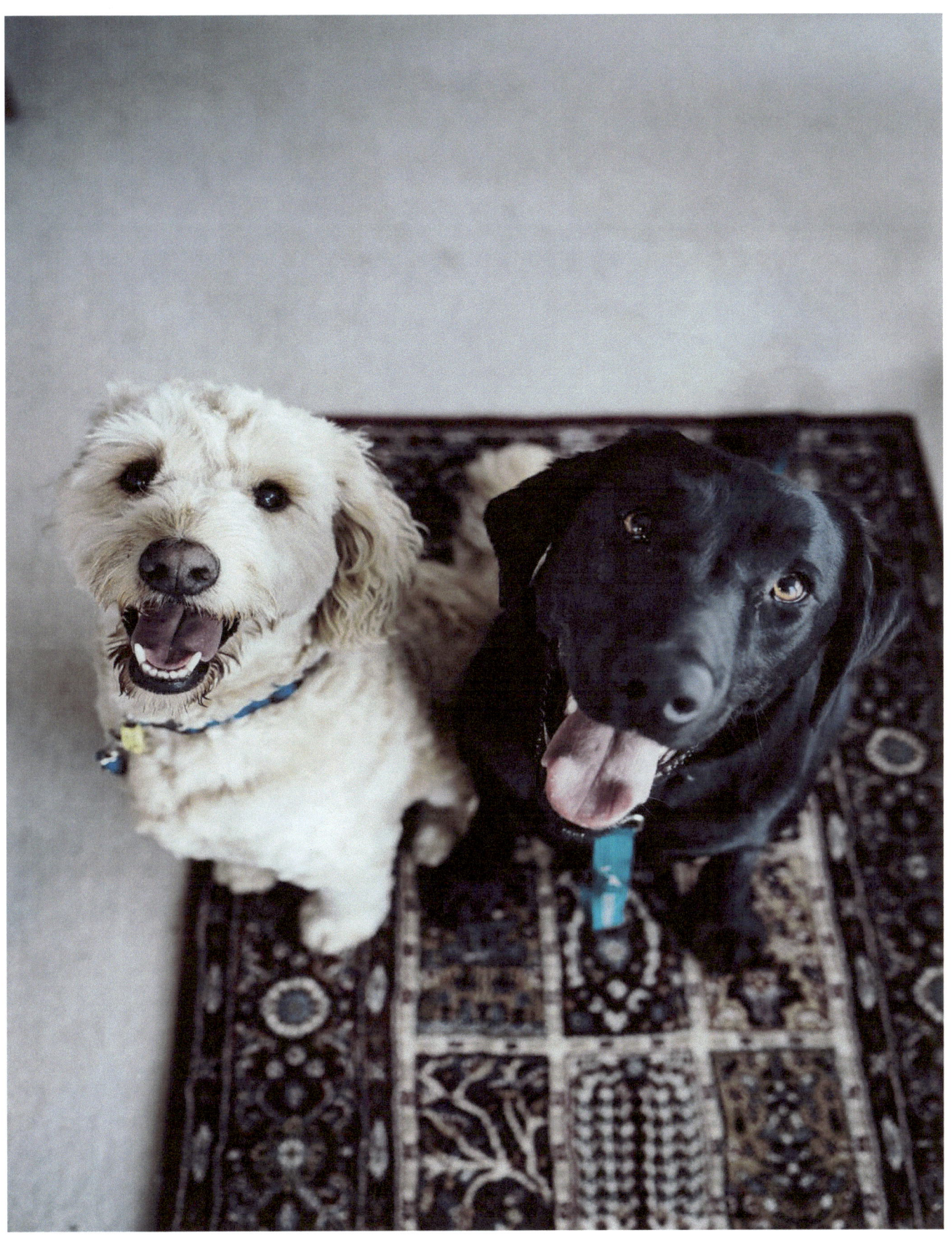

Photographer: Jay Wennington – Sydney, Australia

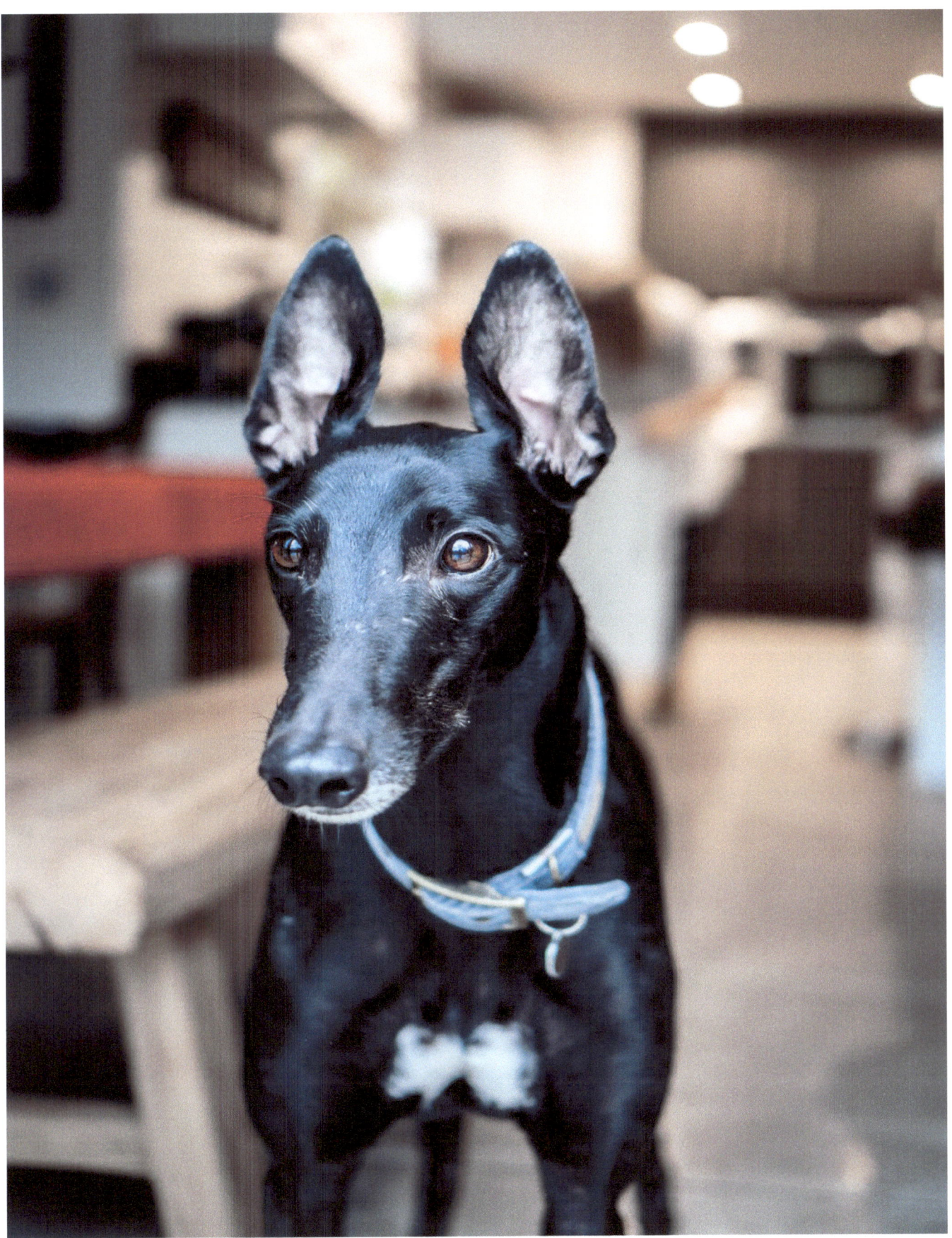

Photographer: Joe Hepburn – Birmingham, UK

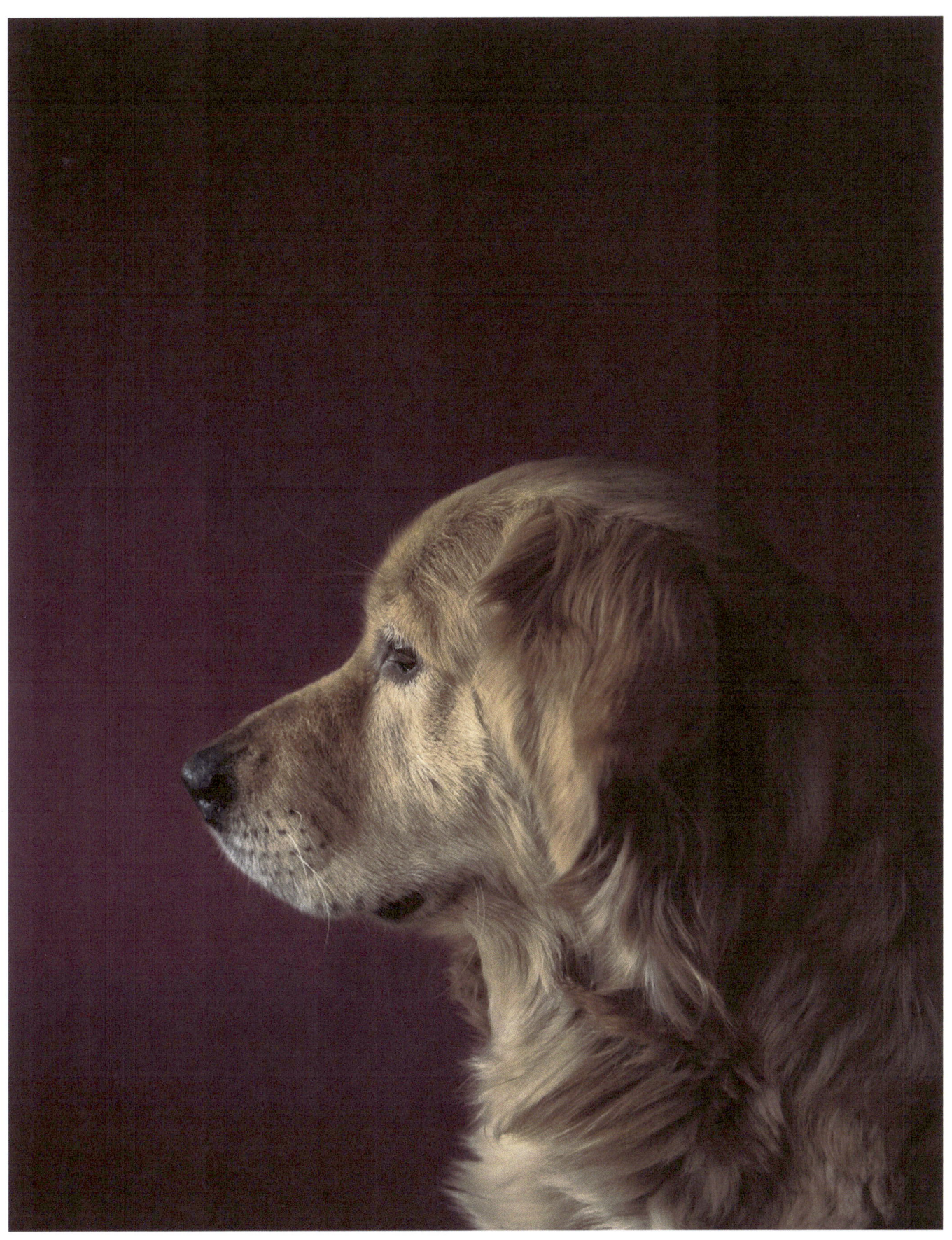

Photographer: Josep Reckziegel – Janov nad Nisou, Czechia

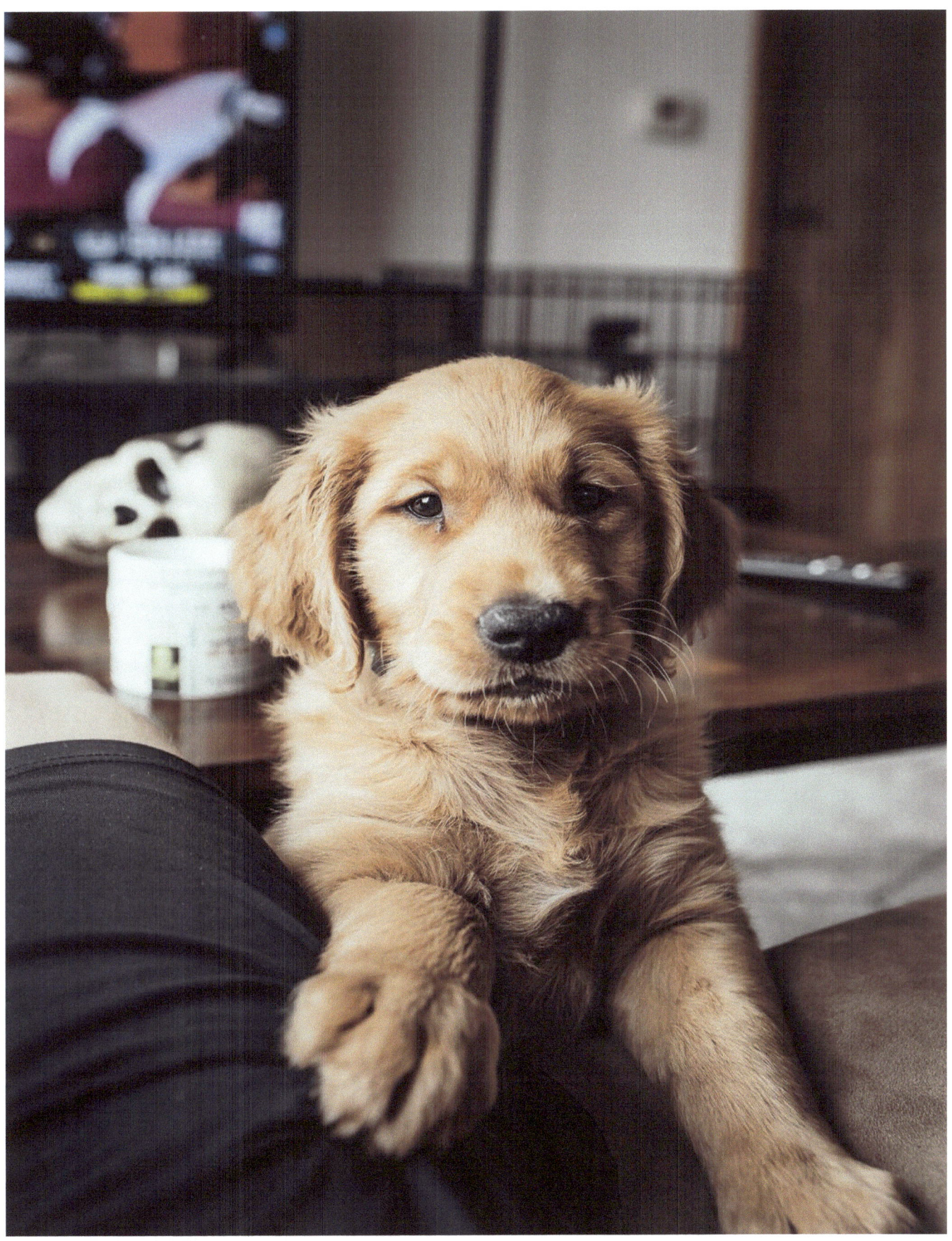

Photographer: Josh Hild

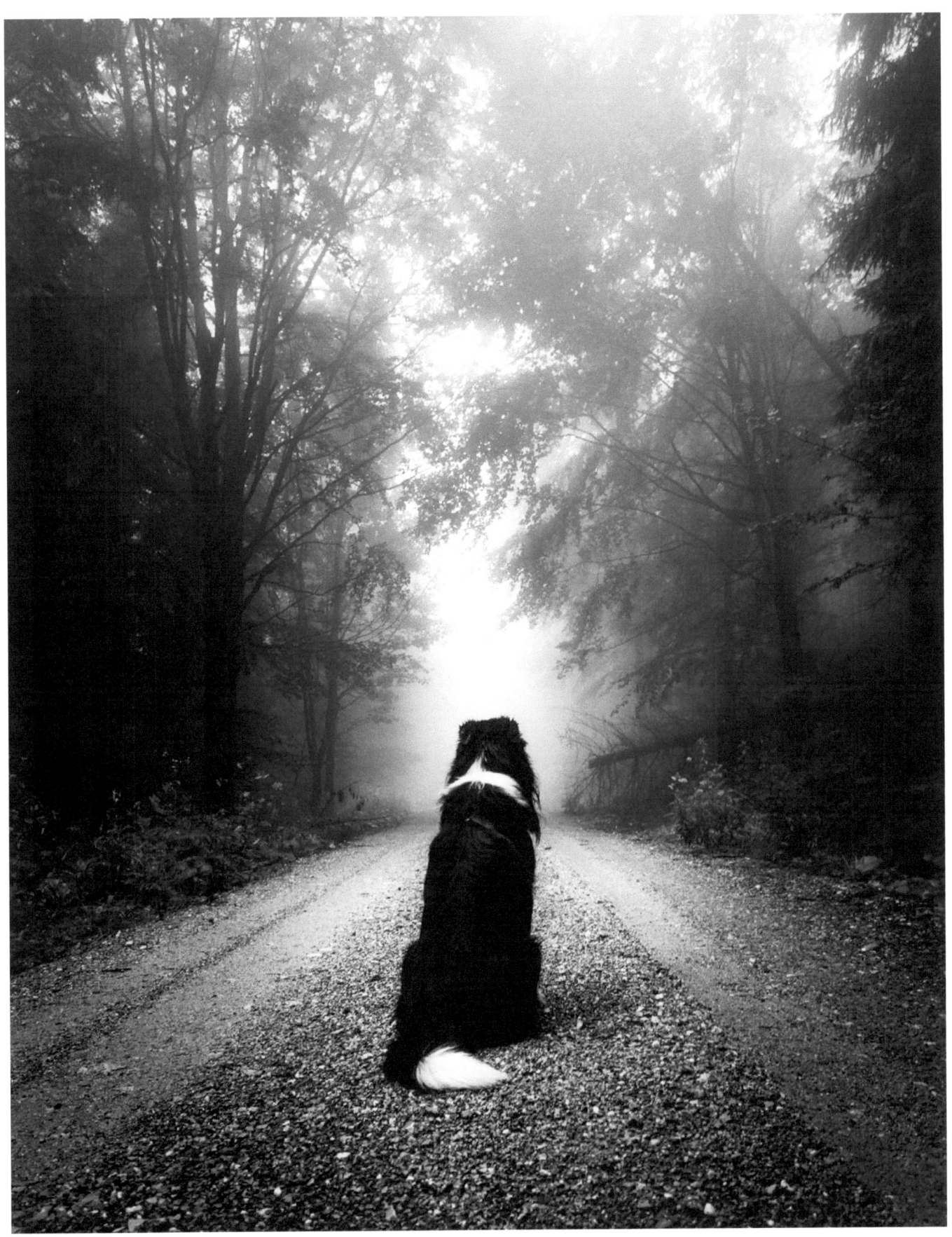

Photographer: Tadeusz Lakota – Czech Republic

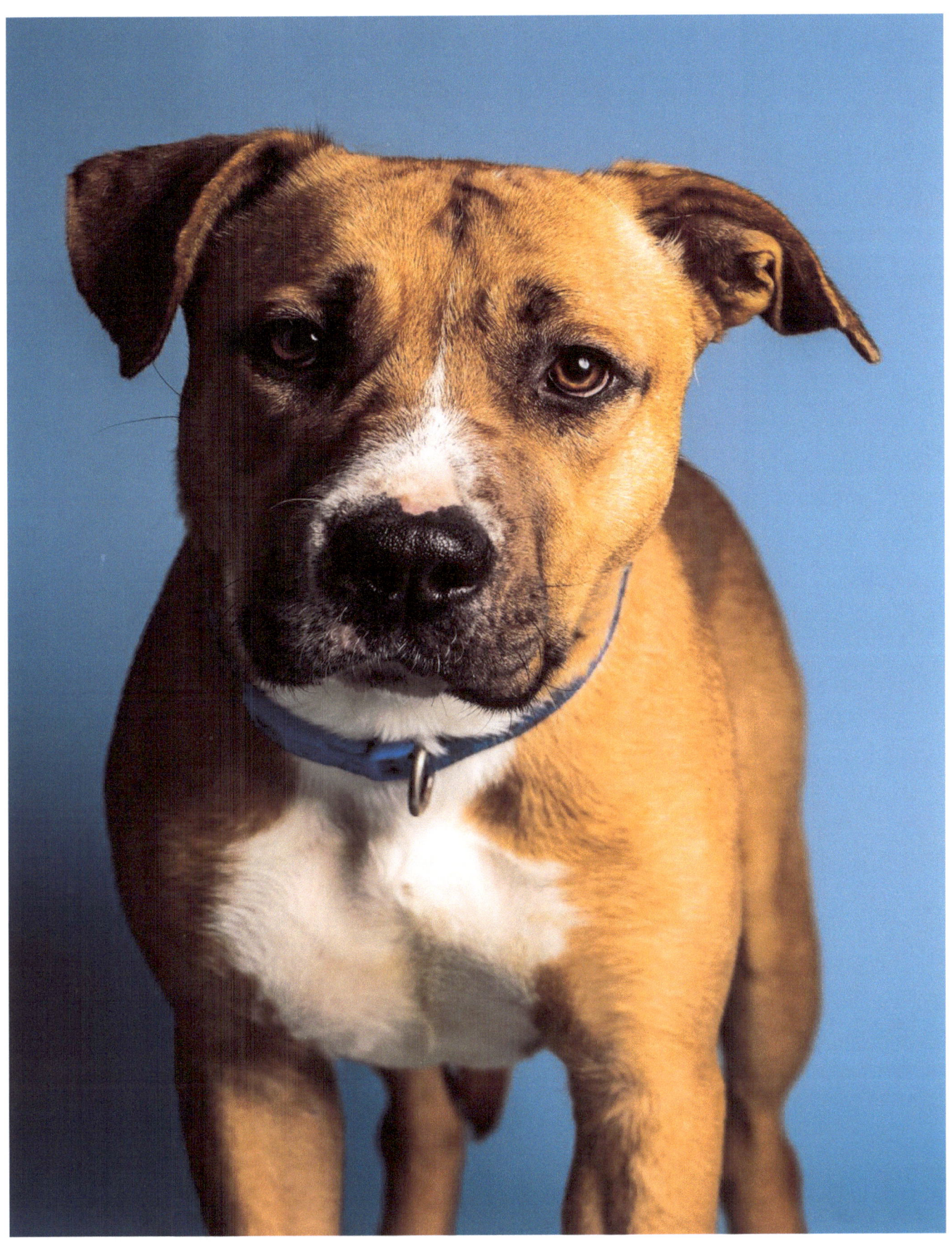

Photographer: Michael G (Rescue Photographer)

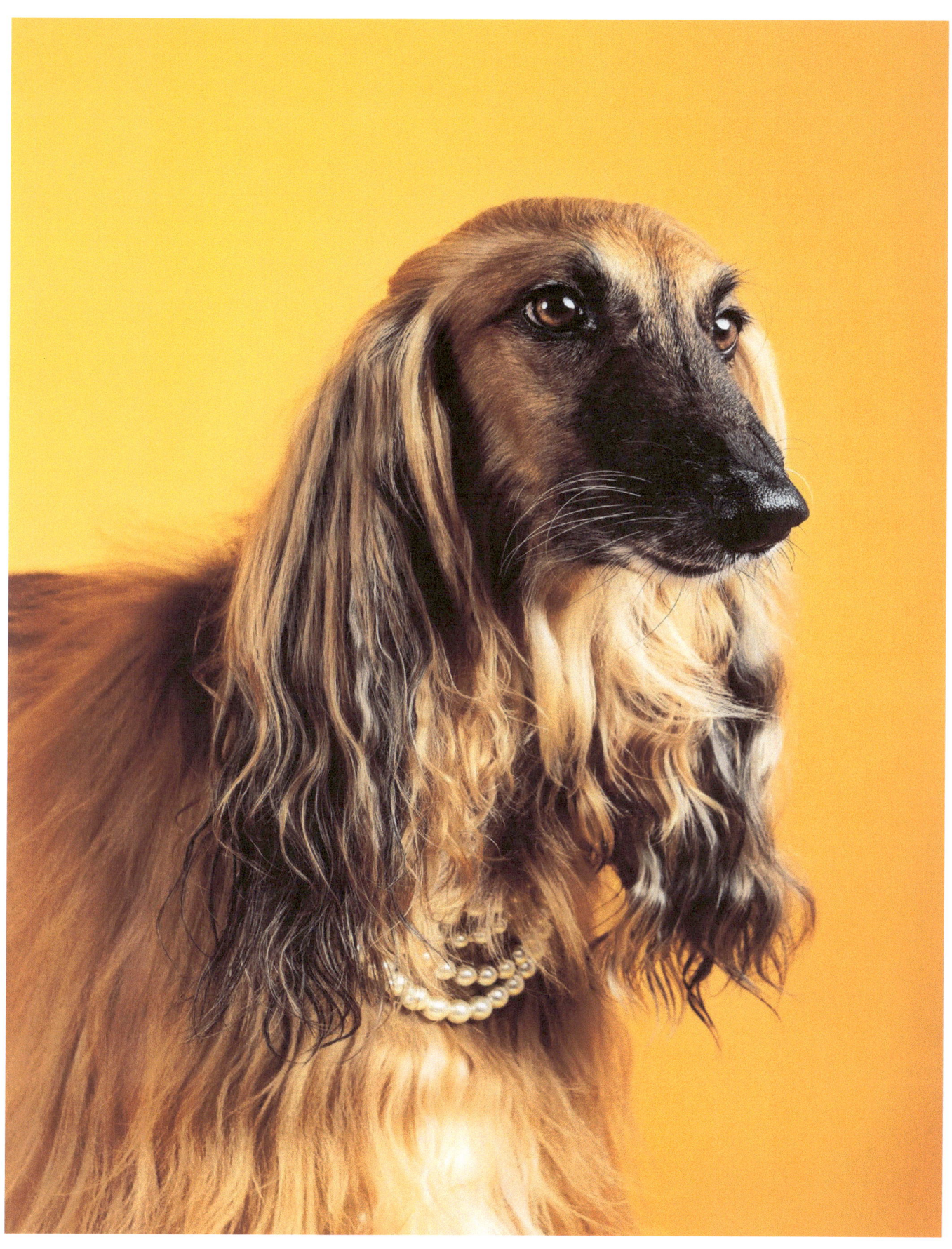

Photographer: Julio Bernal - Mexico

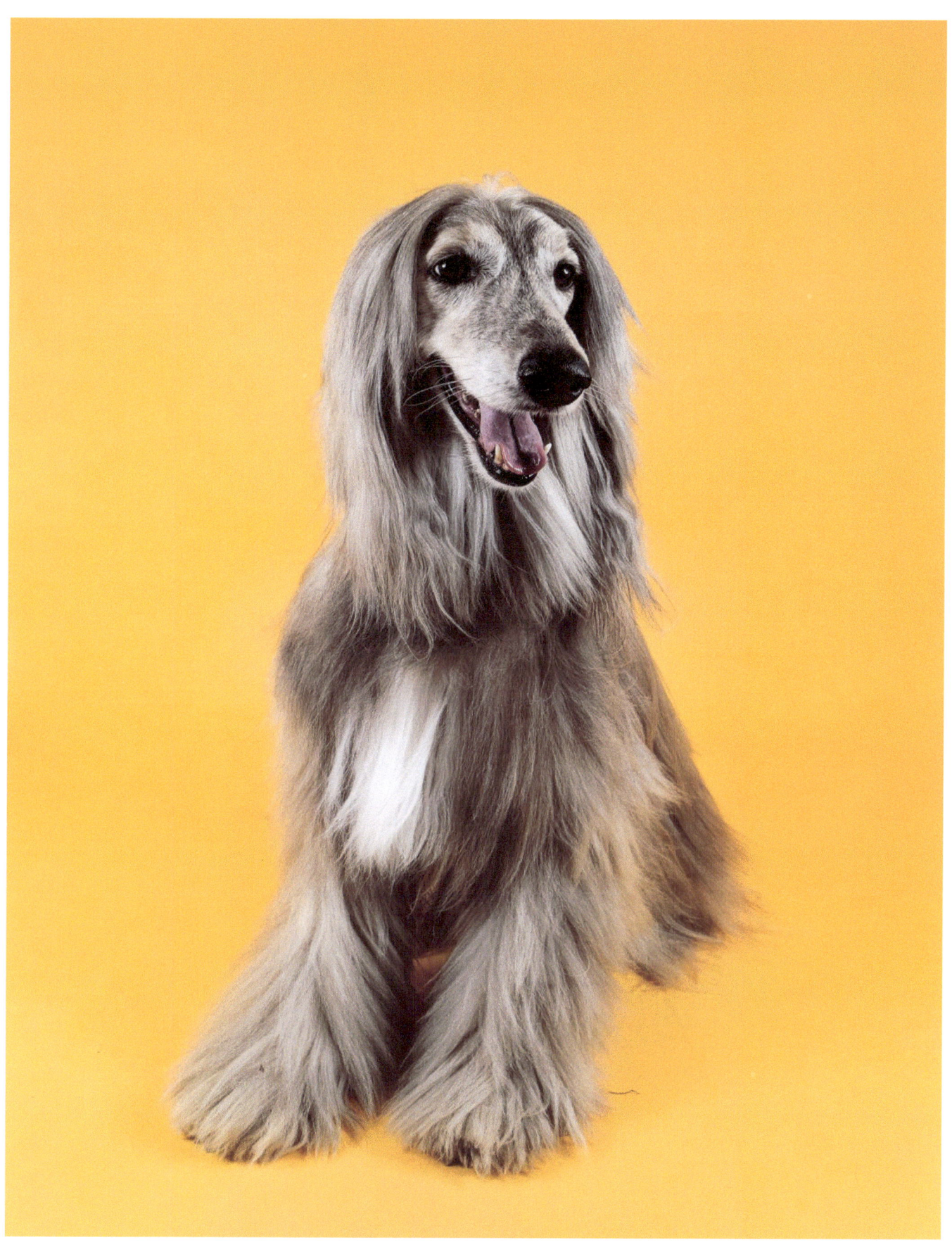

Photographer: Julio Bernal - Mexico

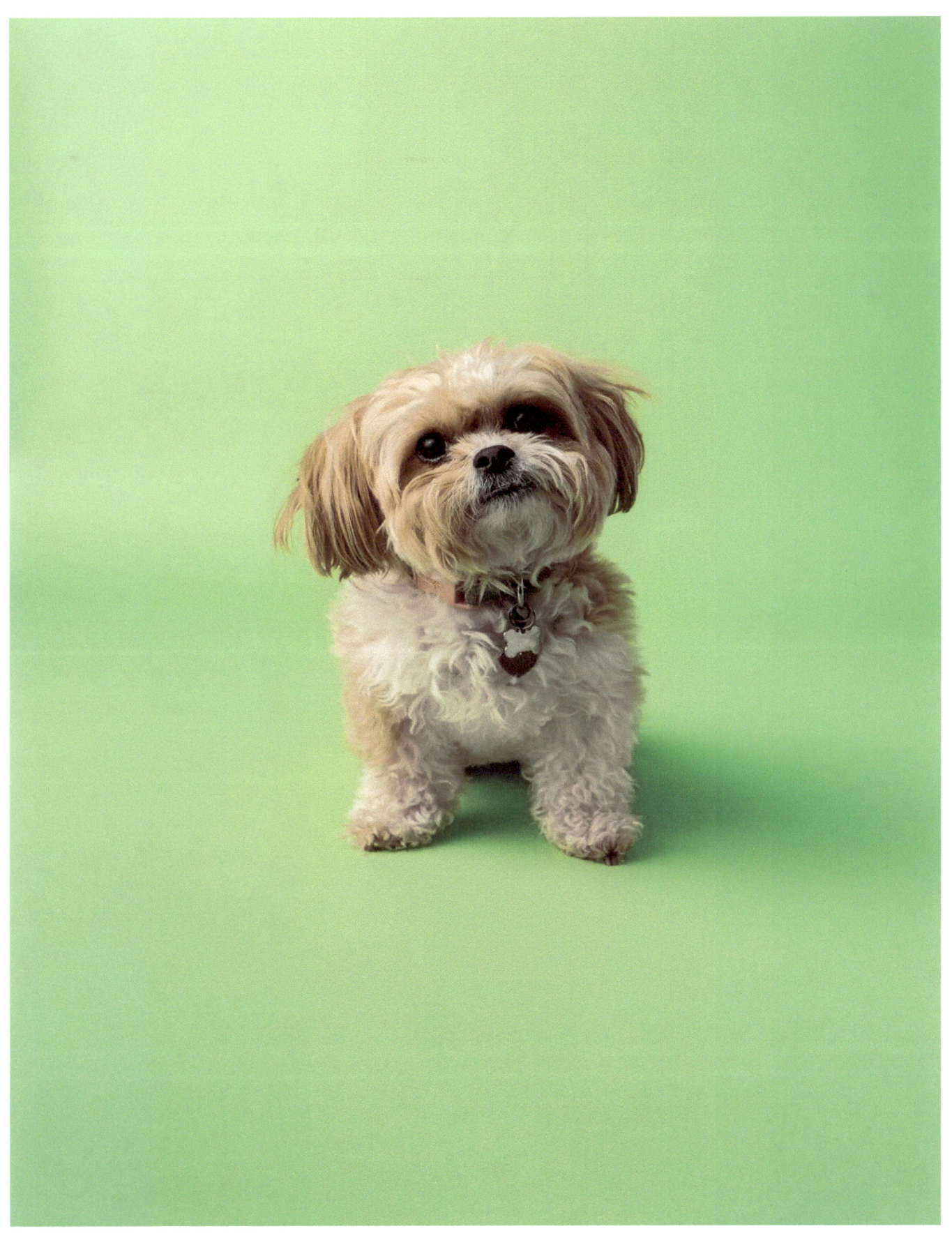

Photographer: Karsten Winegeart – Austin, Texas

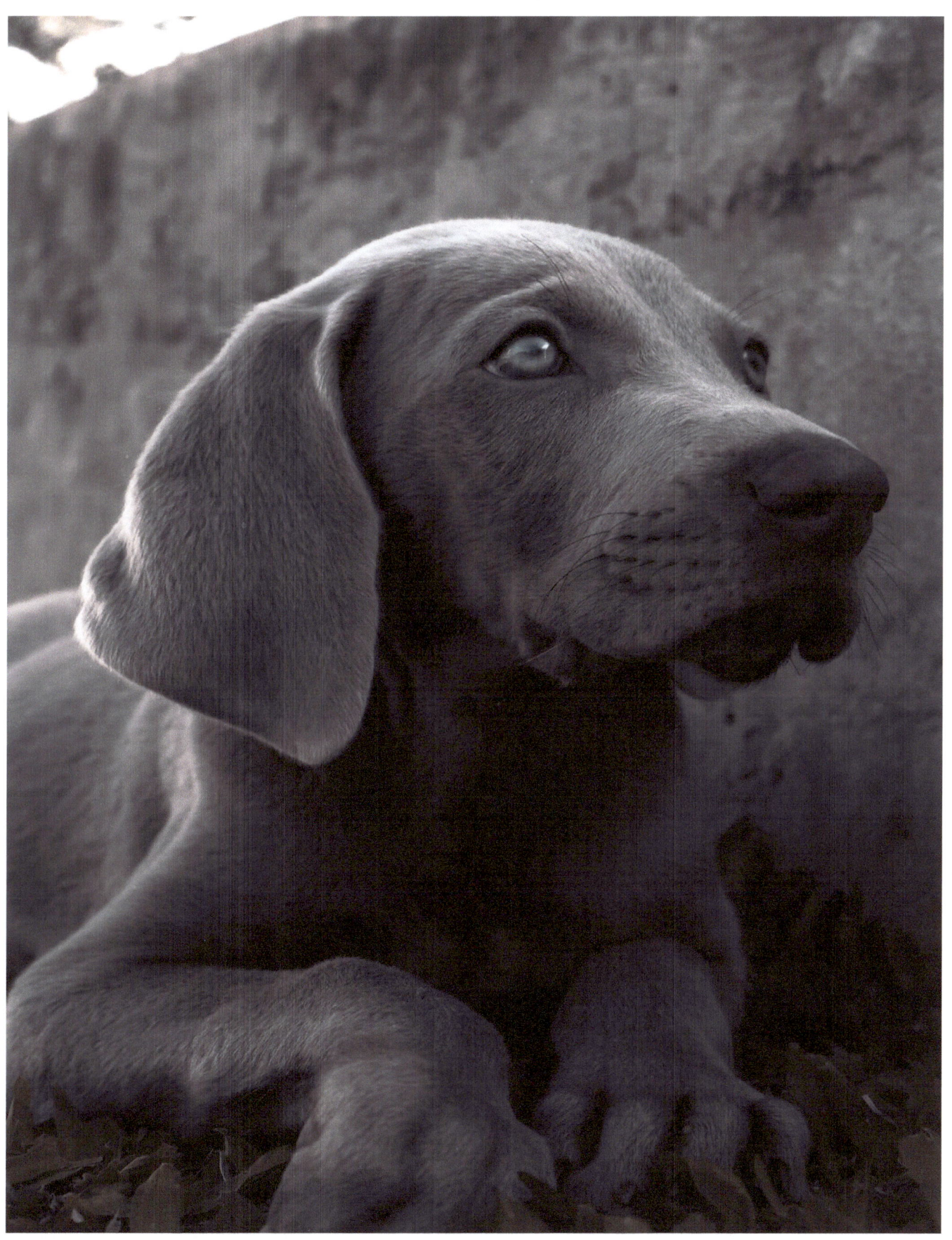

Photographer: Kendall Pena – Costa Rica

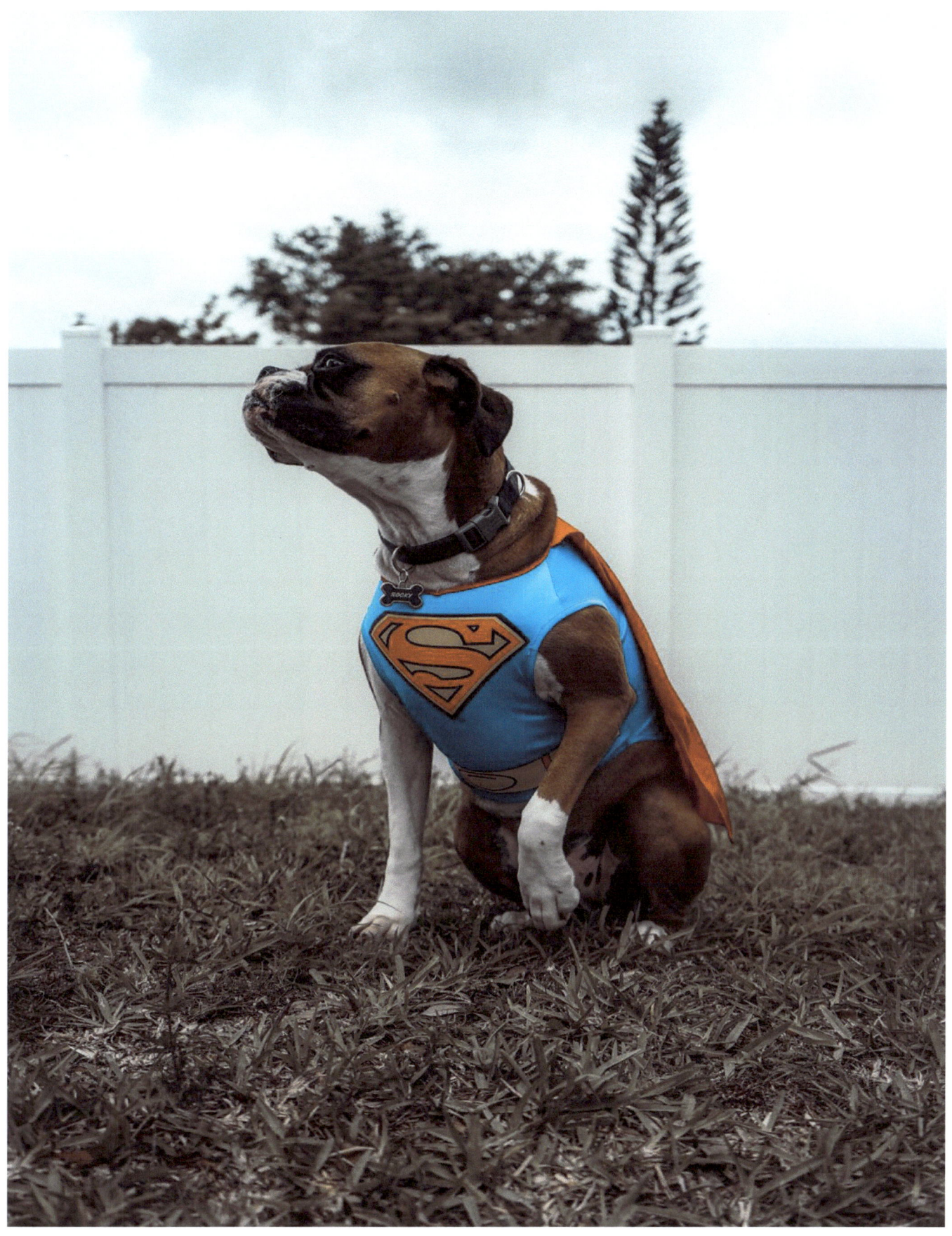

Photographer: Kerwin Elias - Florida

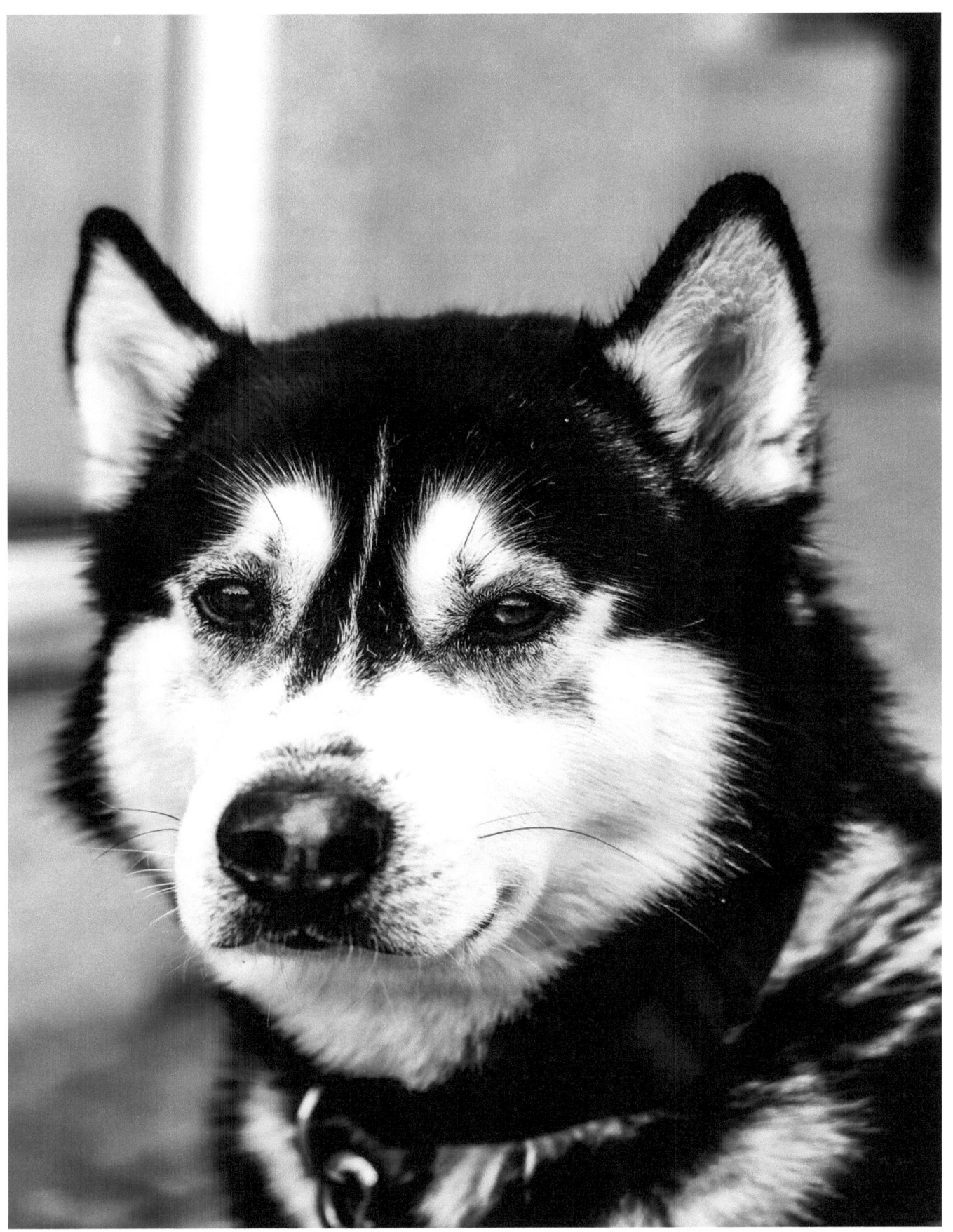

Photographer: Kieran White – Dorset, England

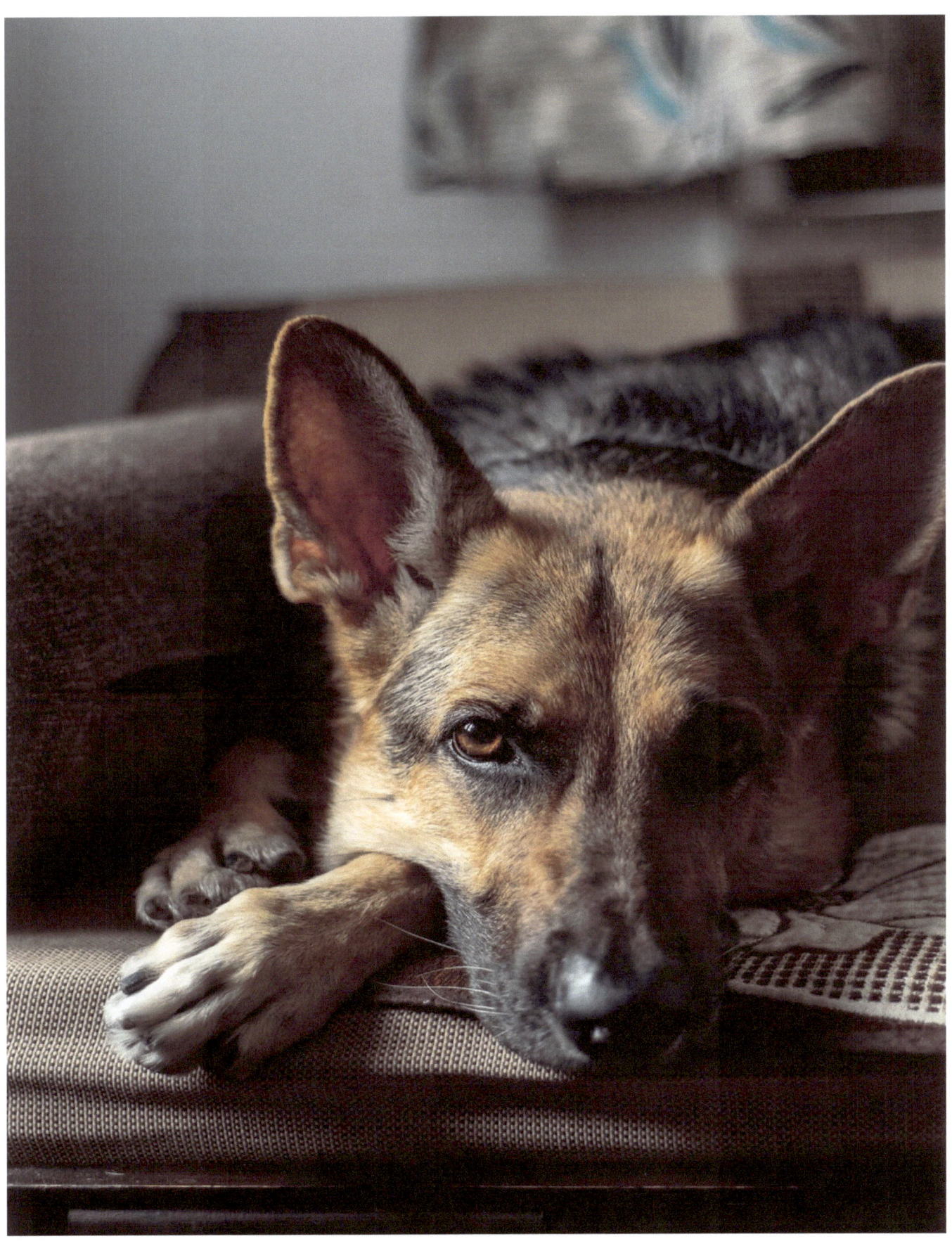

Photographer: Kinshuk Bose

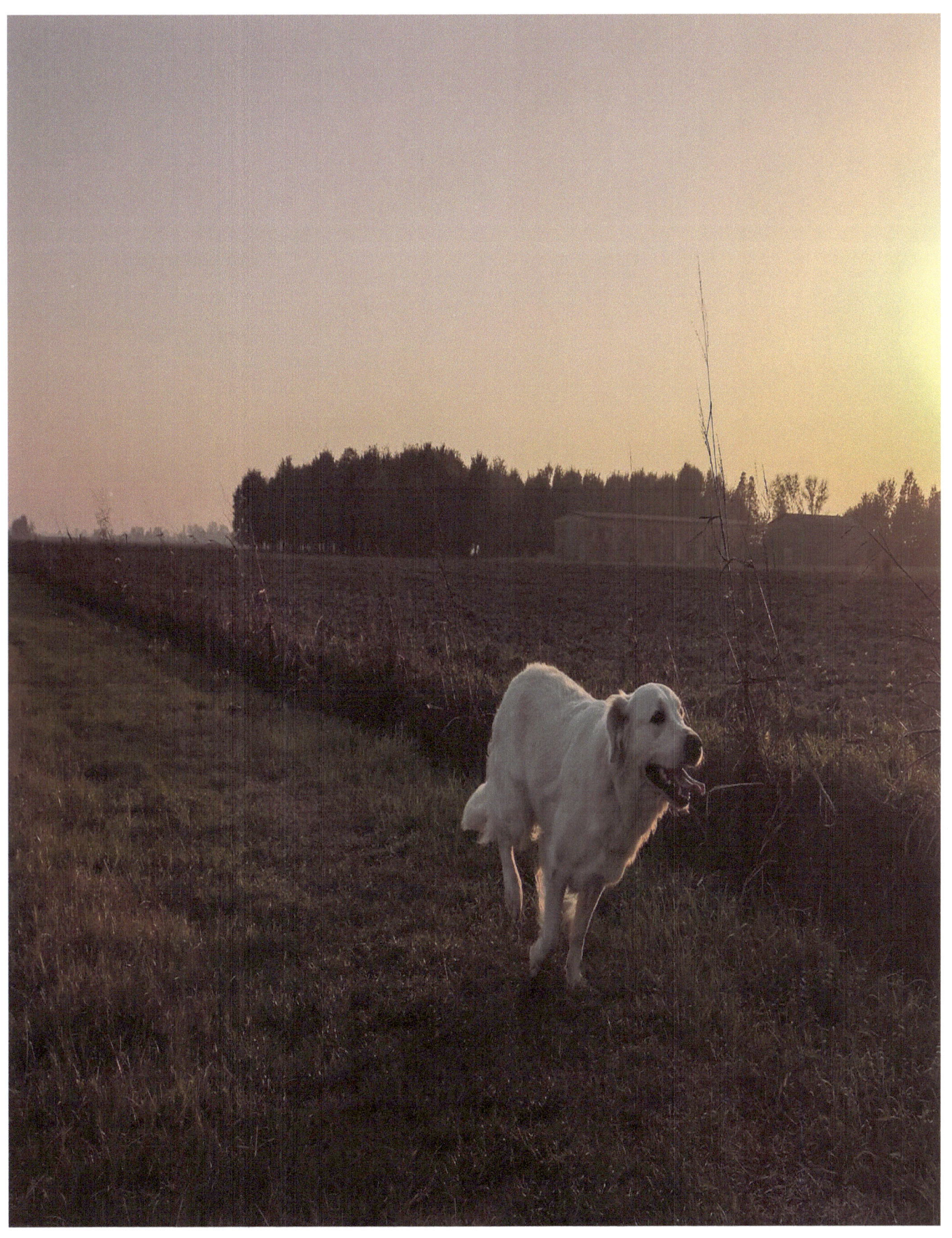

Photographer: Massimo Negrell – Rovigo, Veneto, Italia

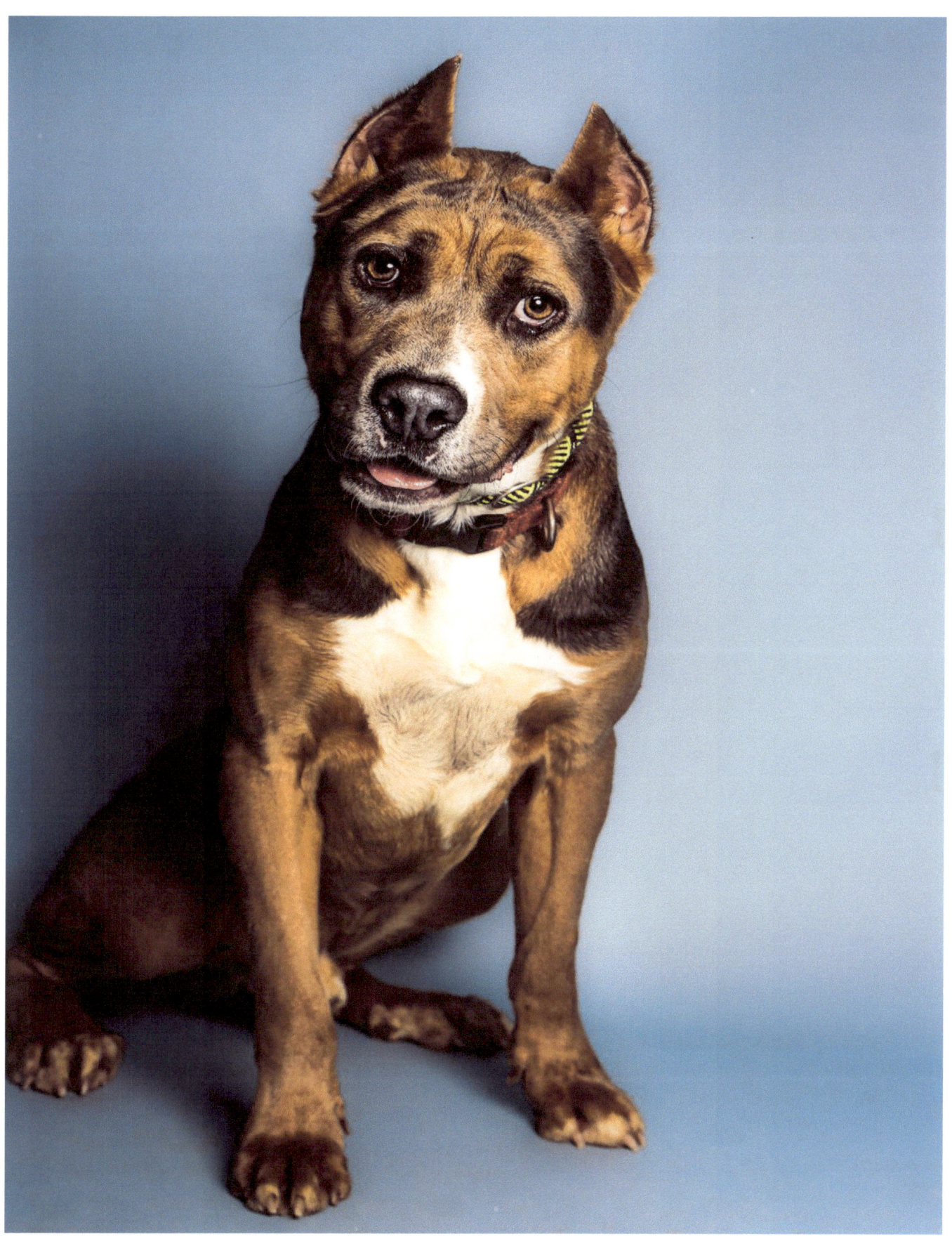

Photographer: Michael G (Rescue Photographer)

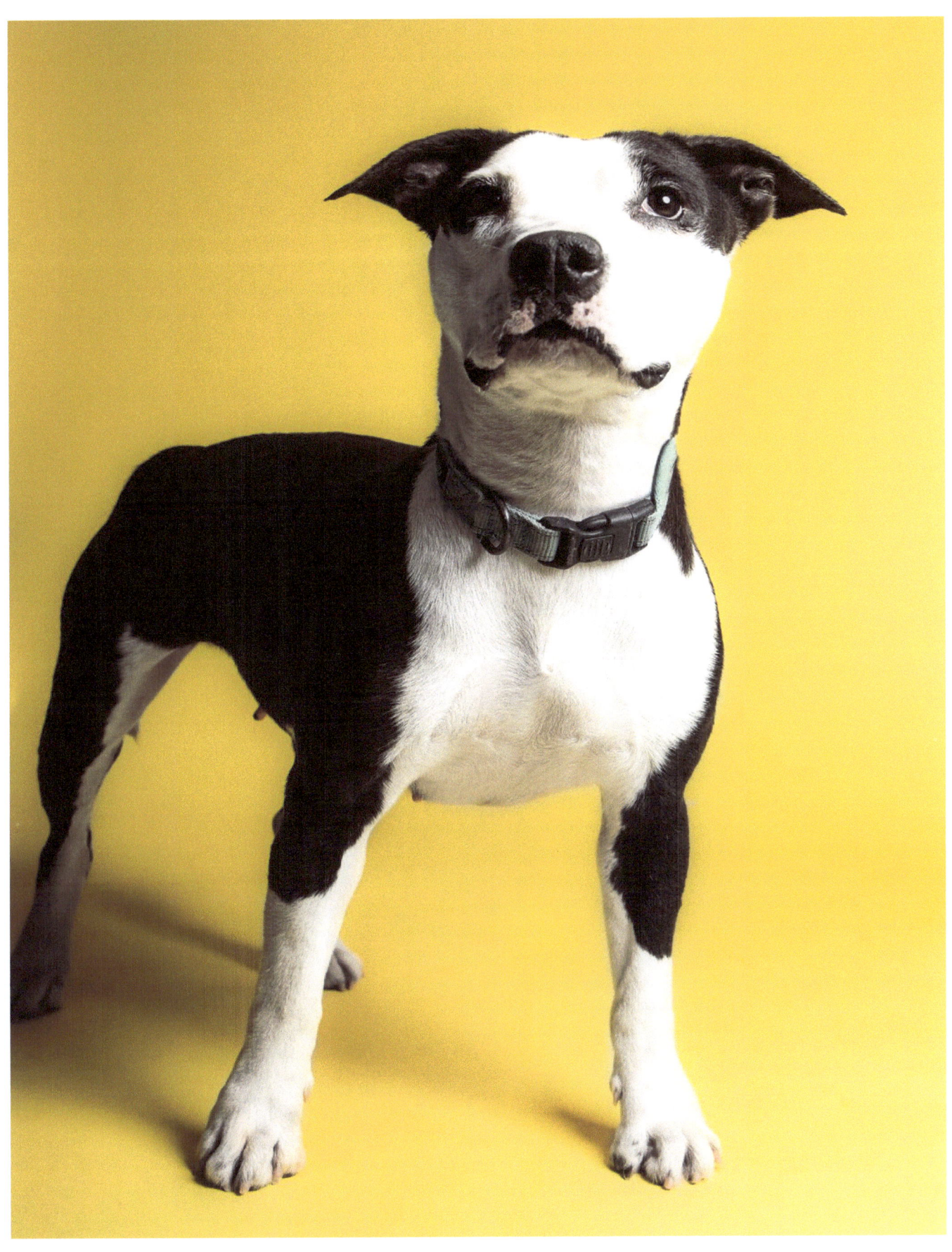

Photographer: Michael G – New Mexico (Rescue Photographer)

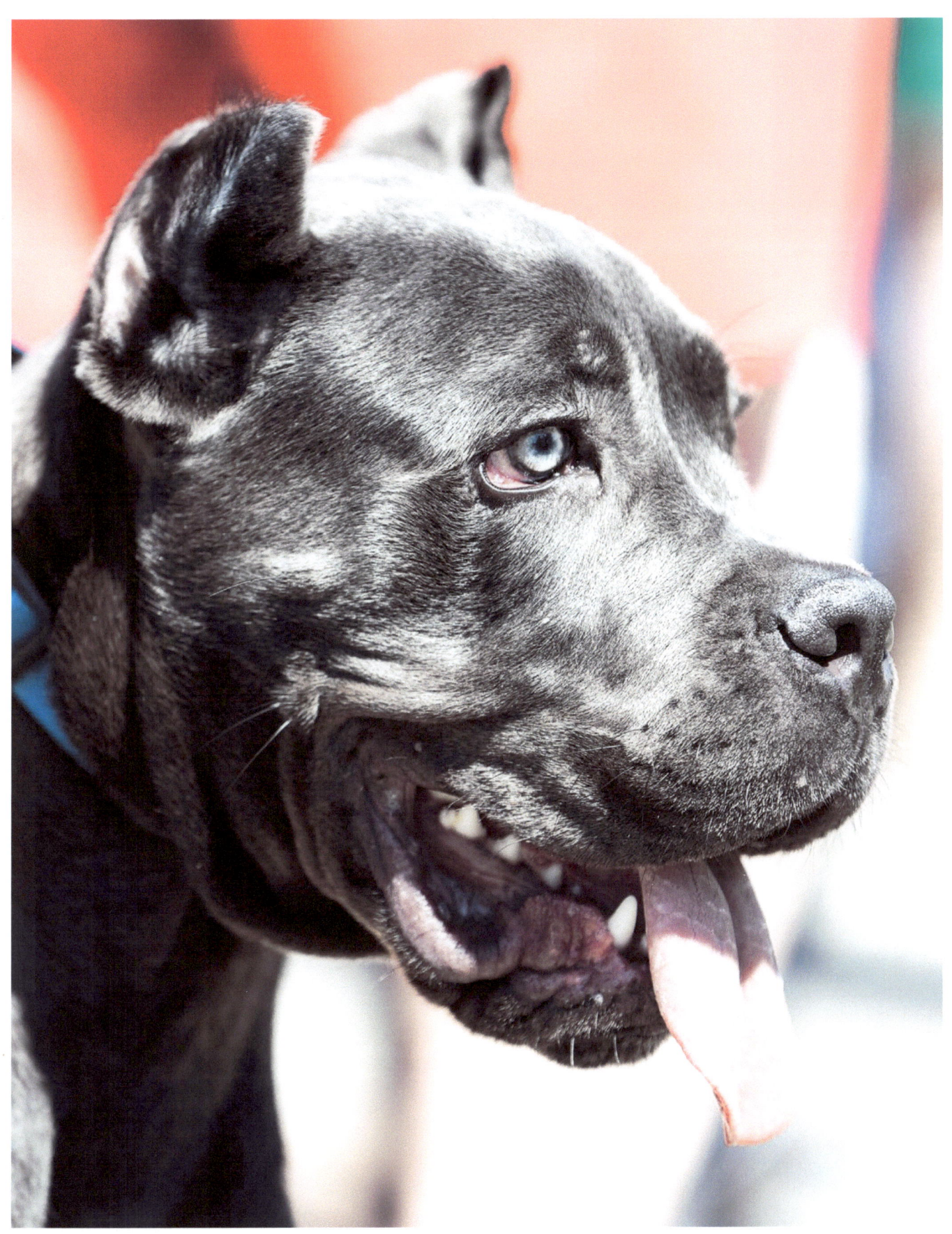

Photographer: Mladen Scekic

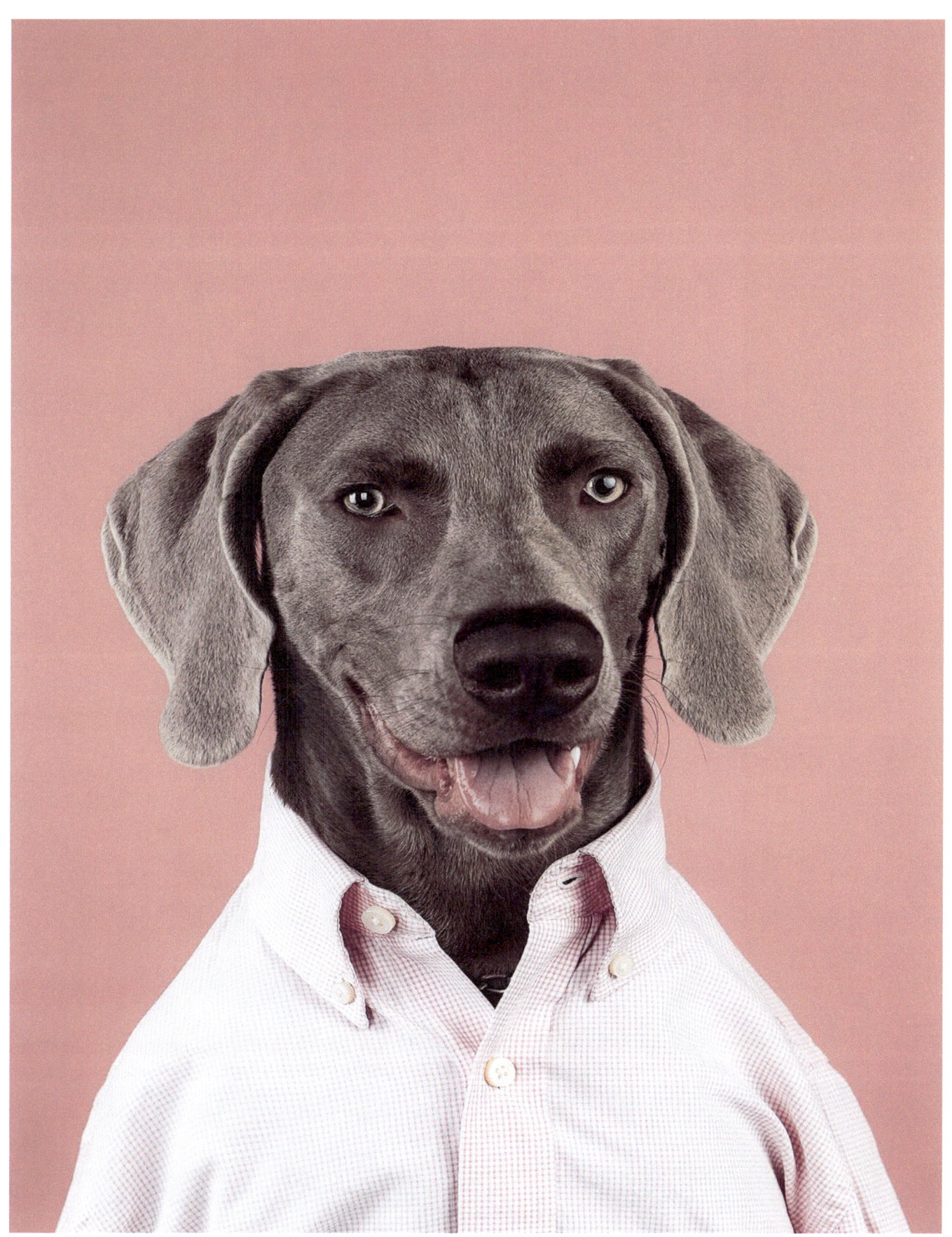

Photographer: Nail Gilfanov – New York

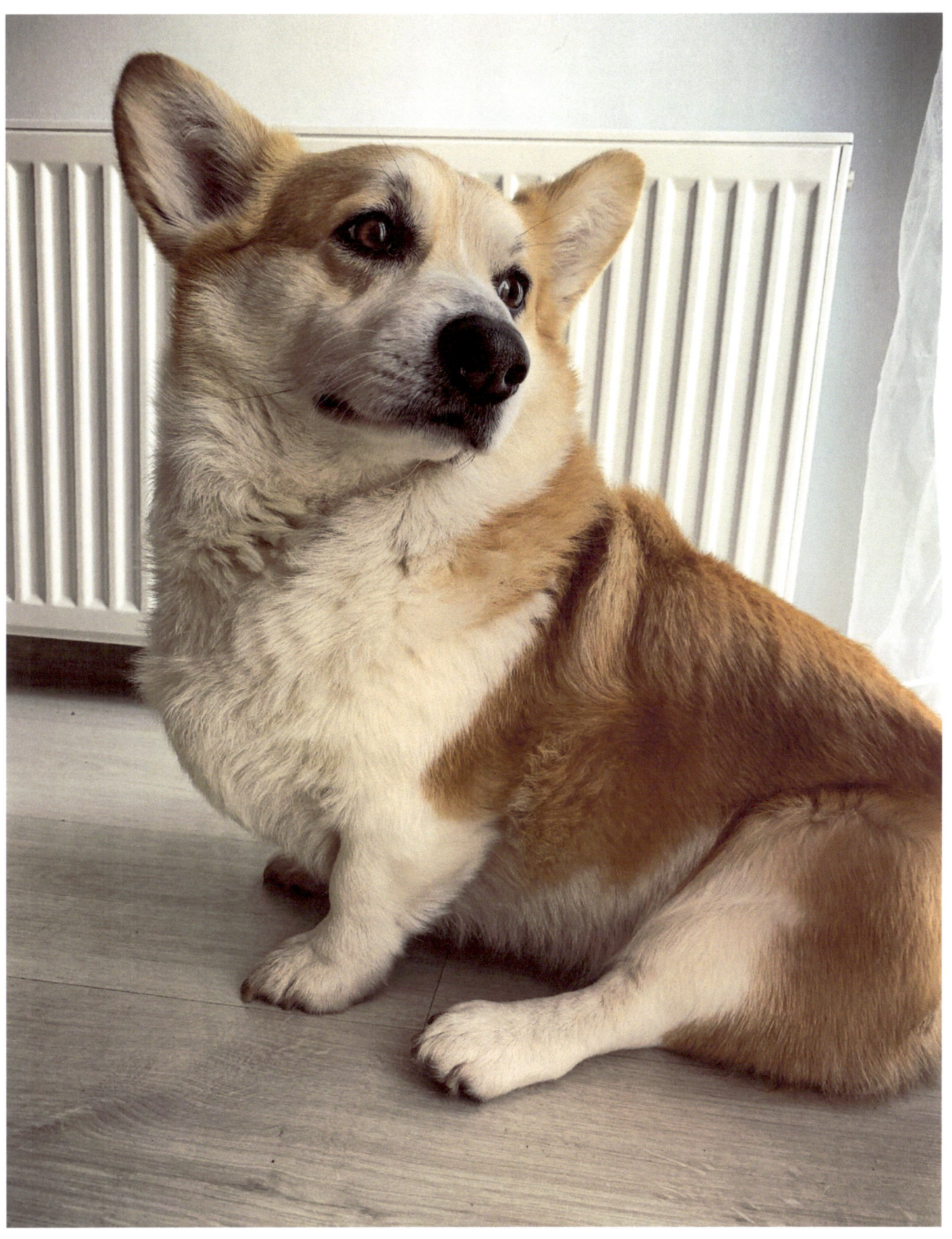

Photographer: Natalia Kvitovska – Calgary, Canada

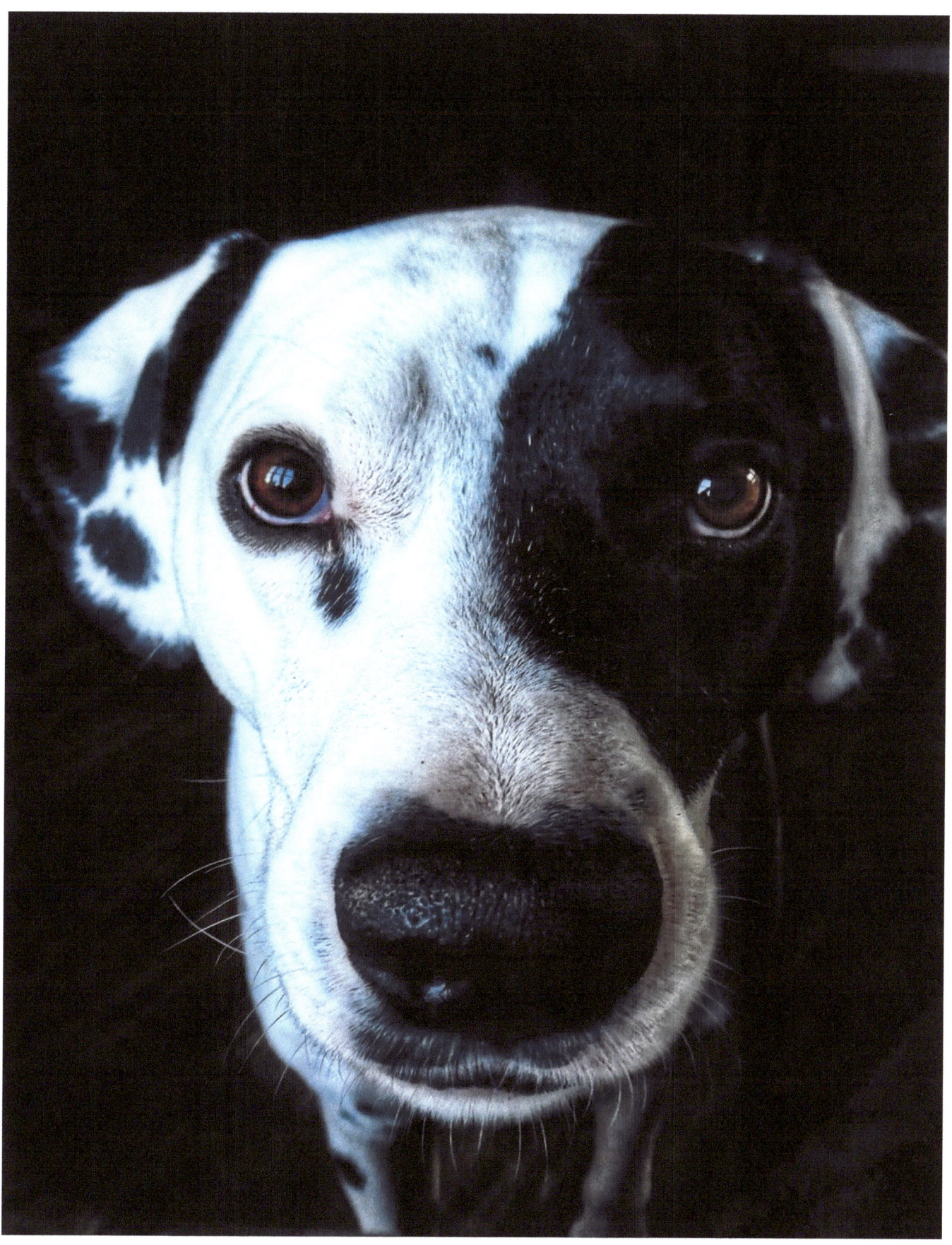

Photographer: Nick Fewings – Bournemouth, UK

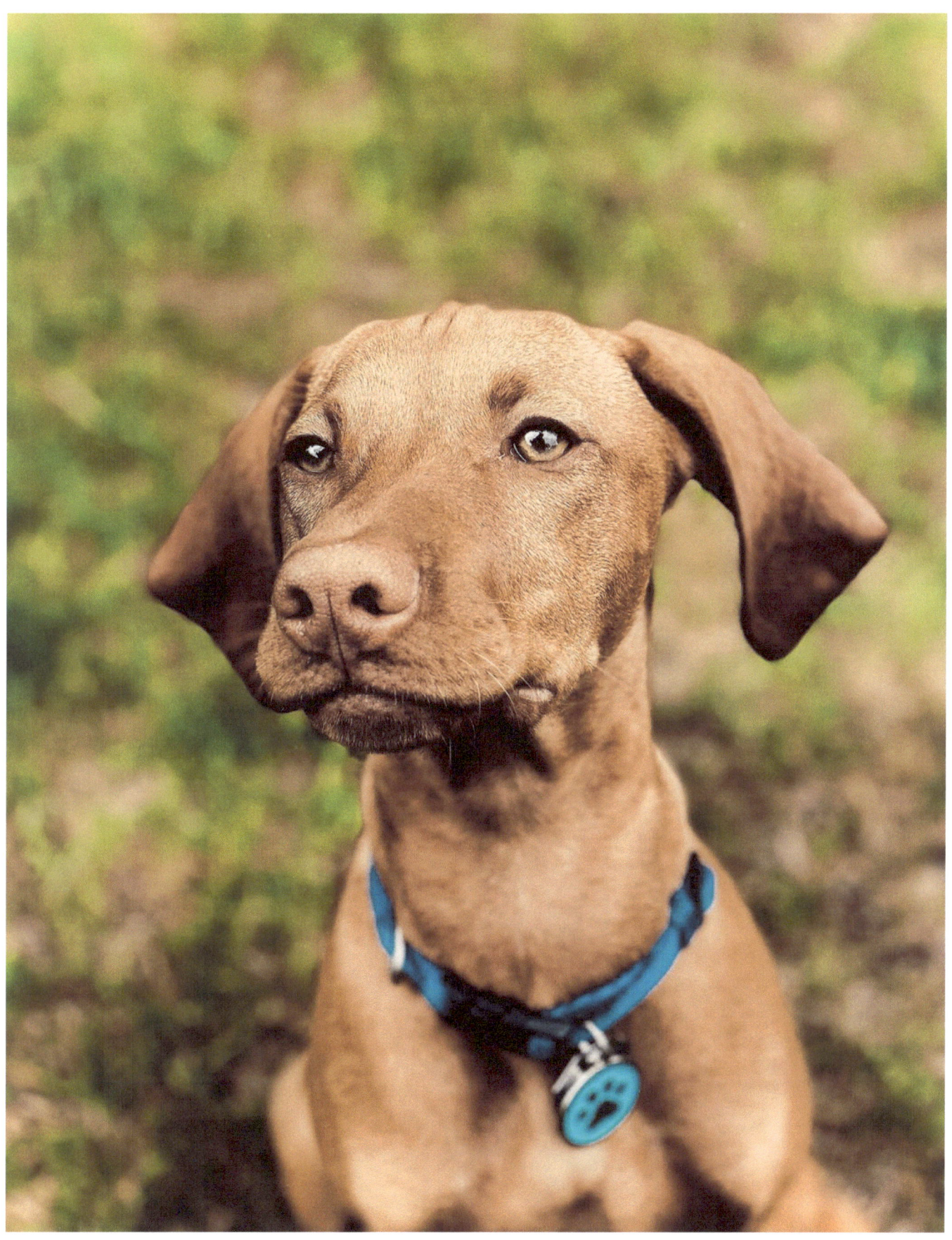

Photographer: Nicholas Falgetelli – Blaine, Minnesota

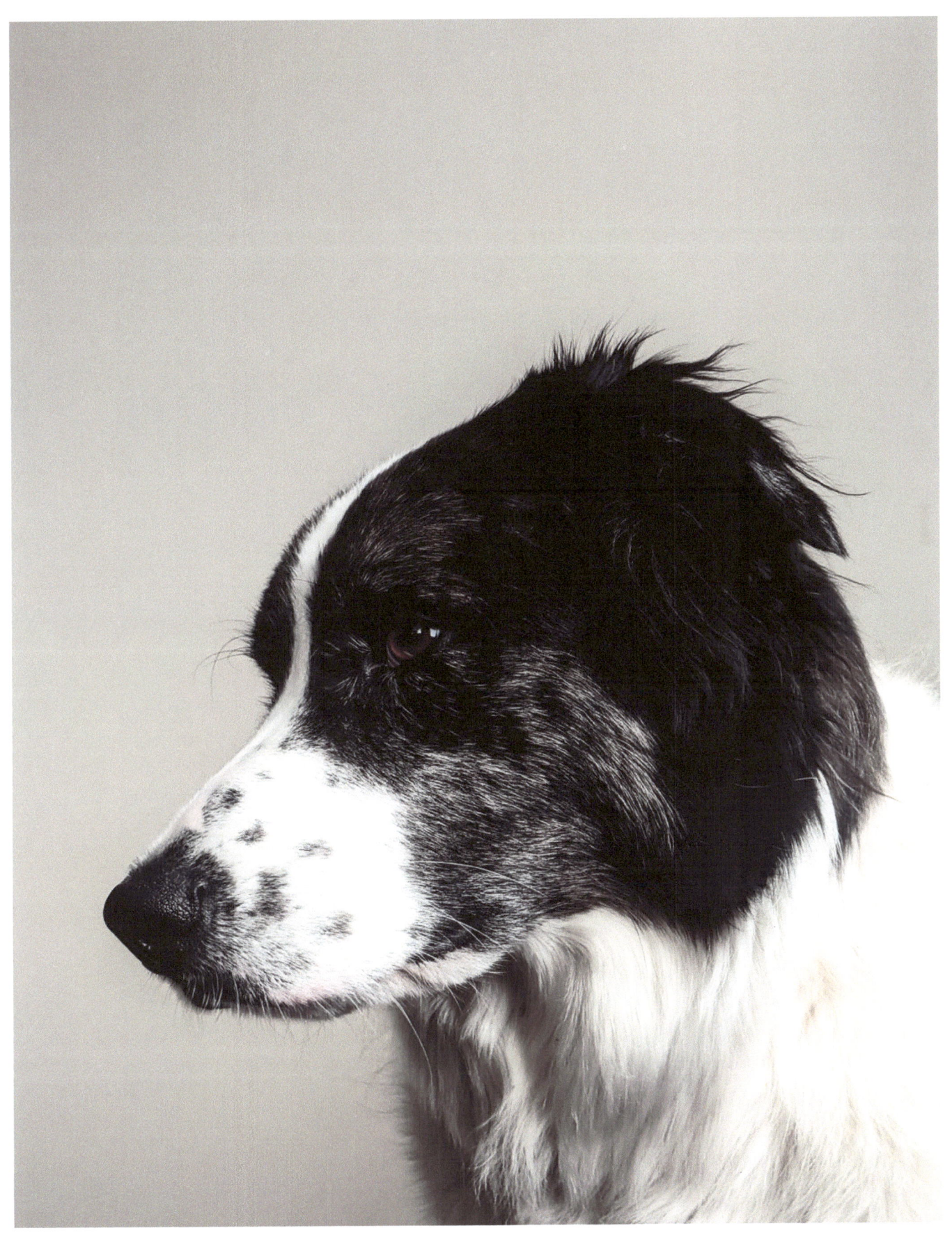

Photographer: Omar Flores – Toronto, Ontario, Canada

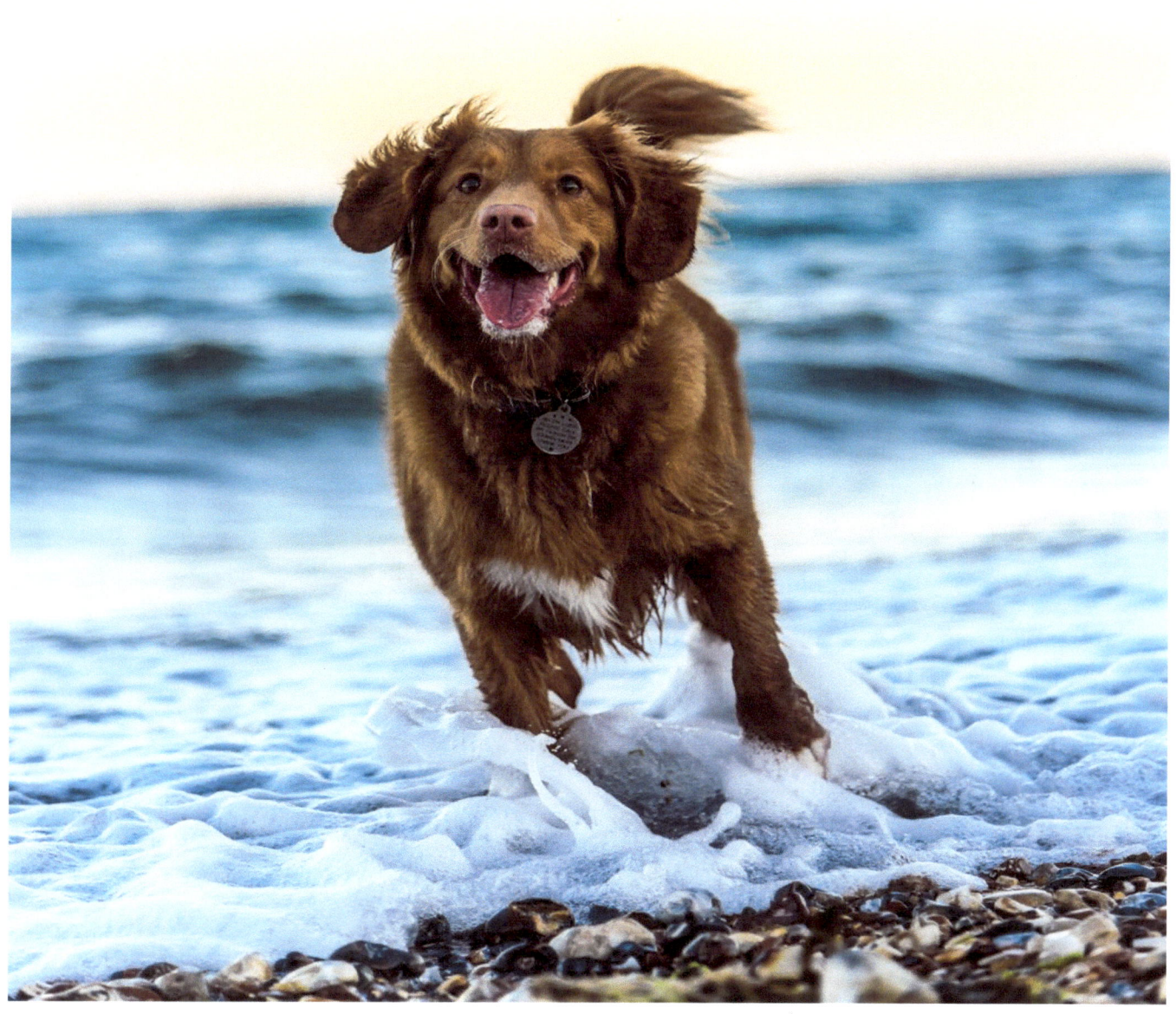

Photographer: Oscar Sutton – UK

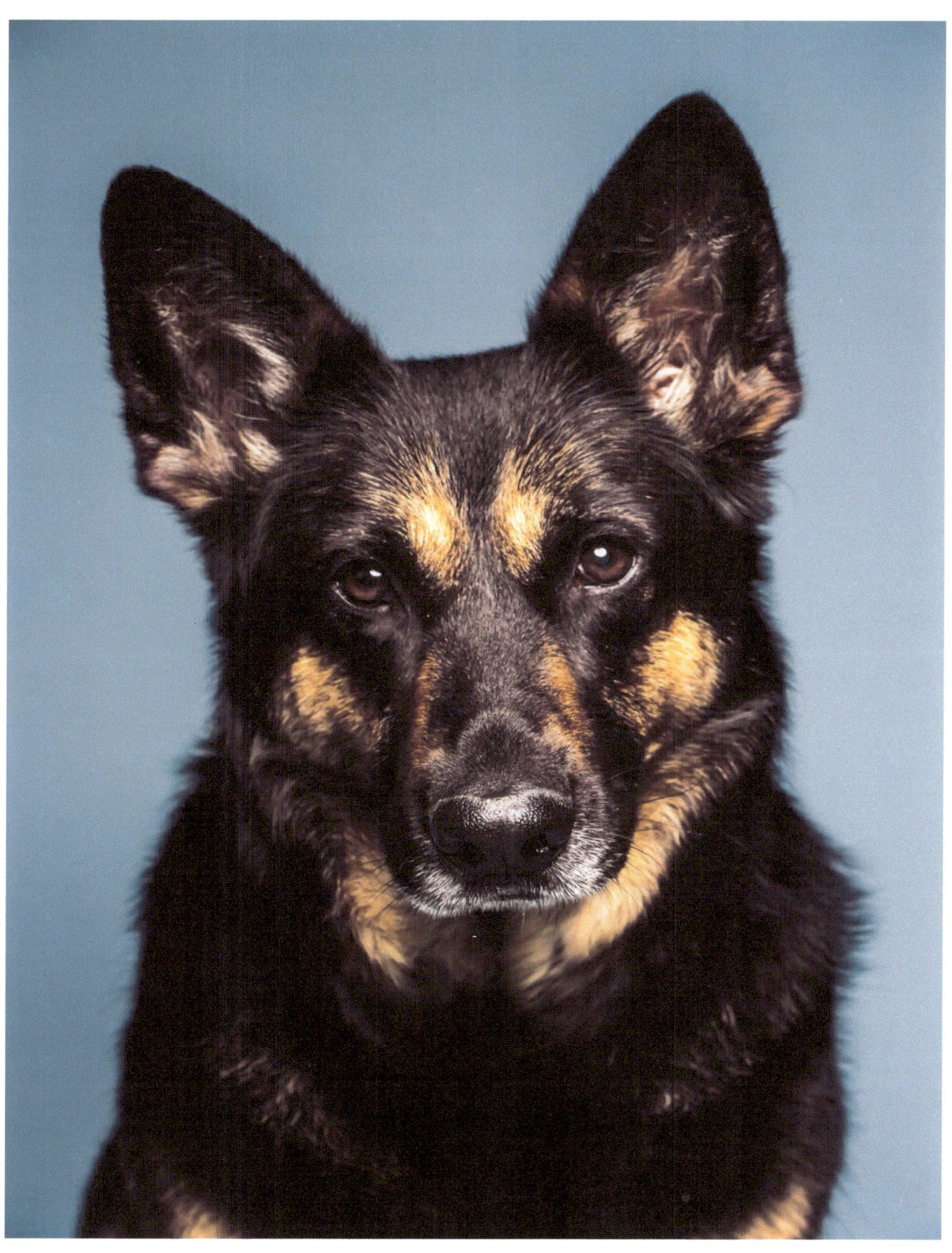

Photographer: Michael G – New Mexico – (Rescue Photographer)

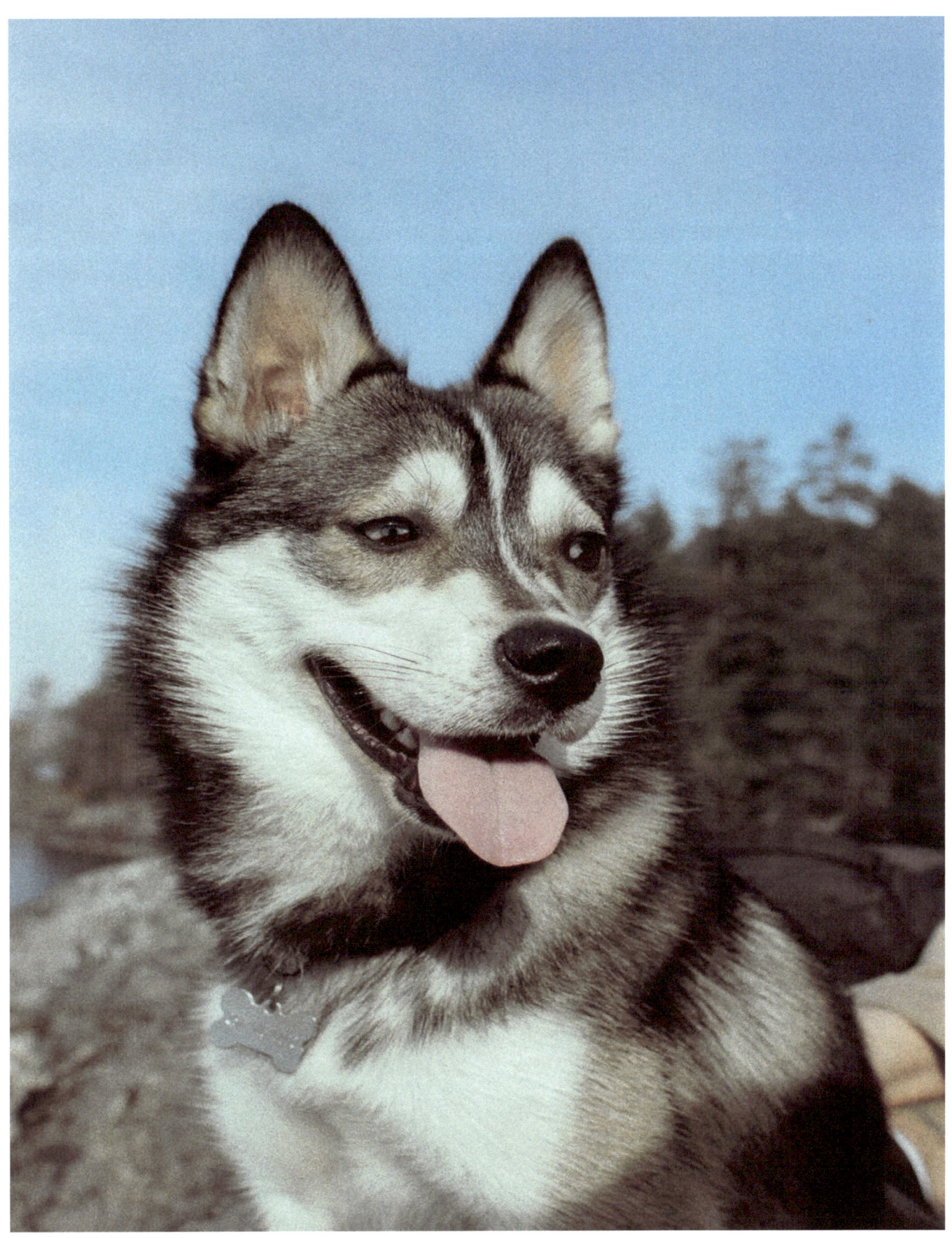

Photographer: Philippe Nick

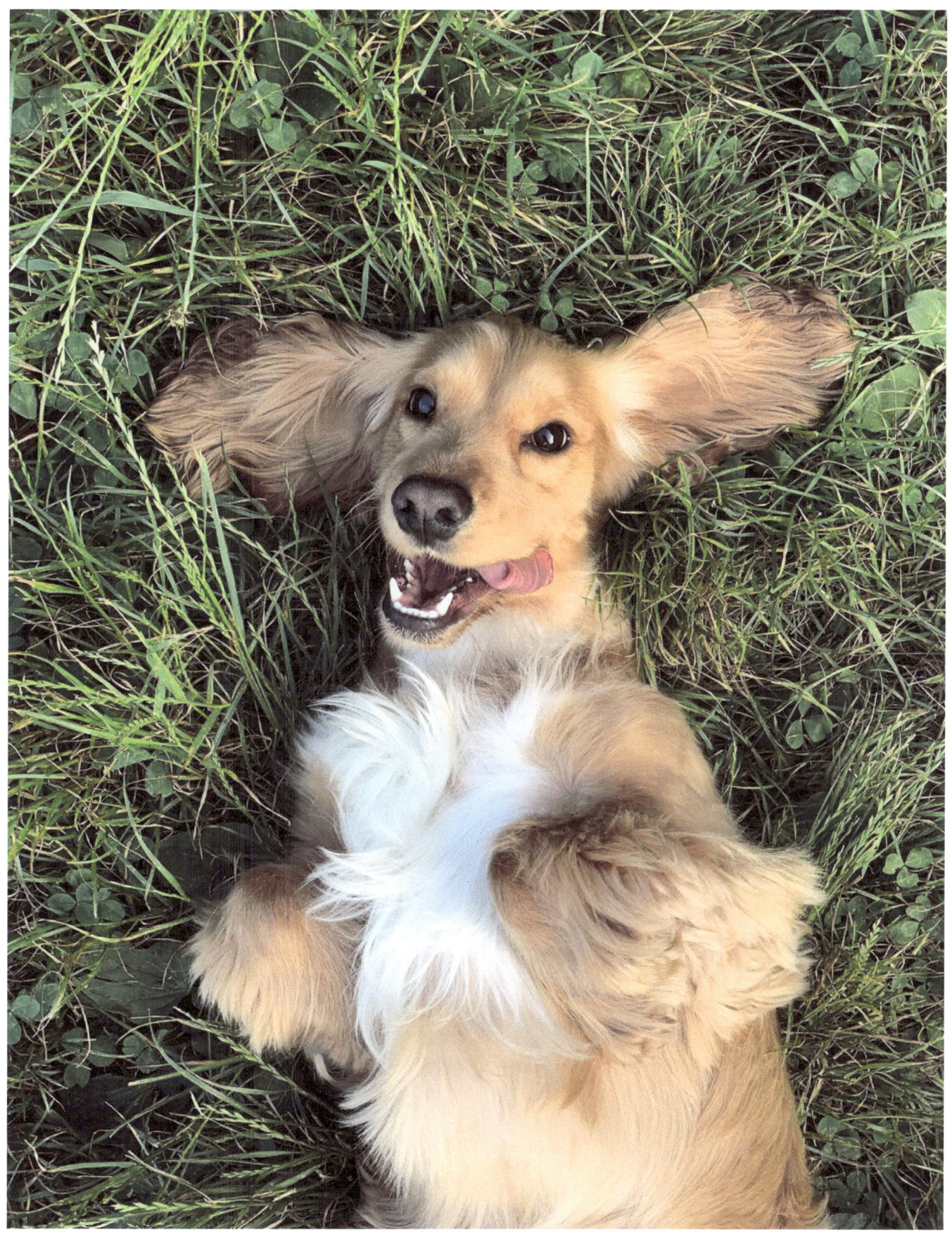

Photographer: Ralu Gal - Romania

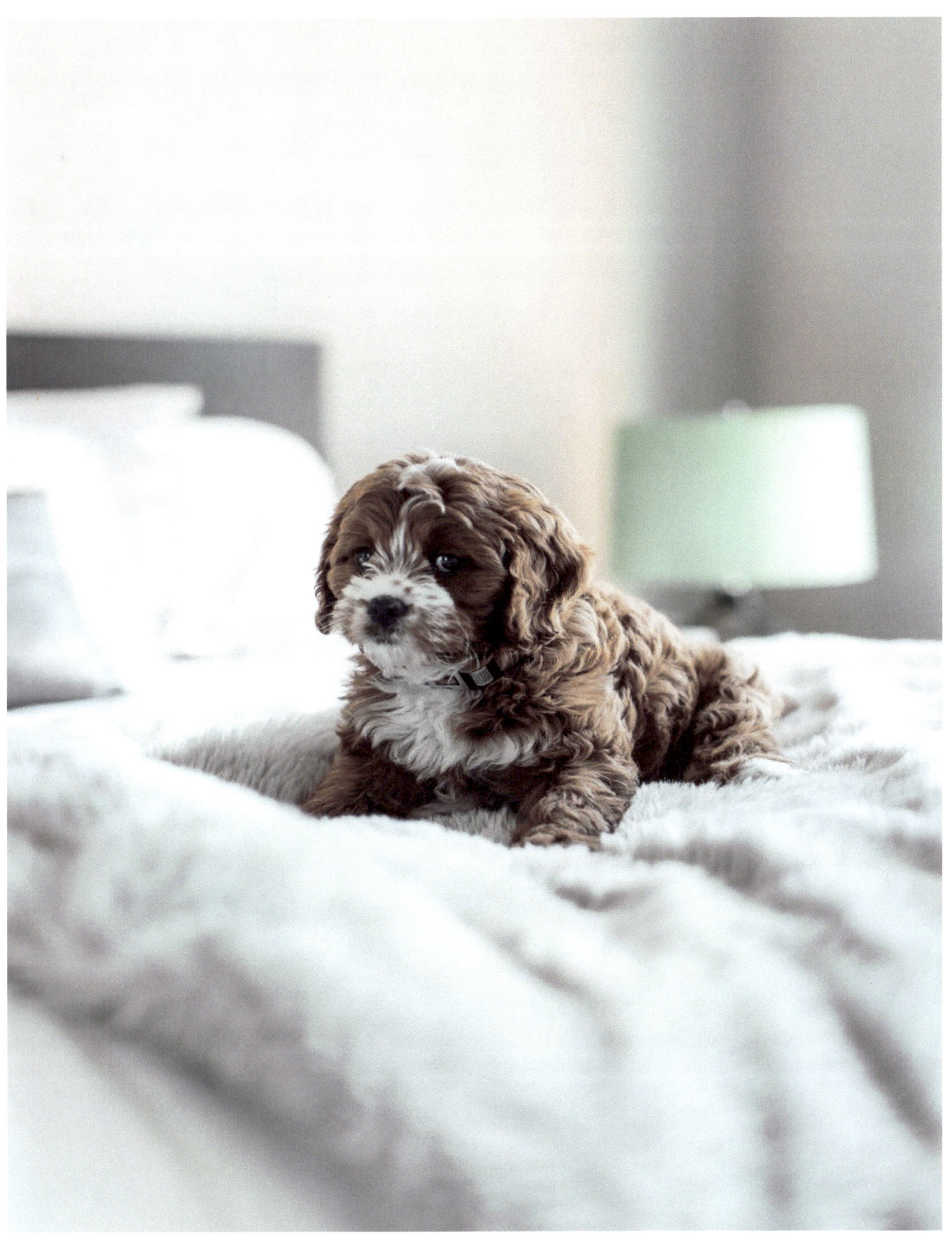
Photographer: Roberto Nickson – Los Angeles, CA

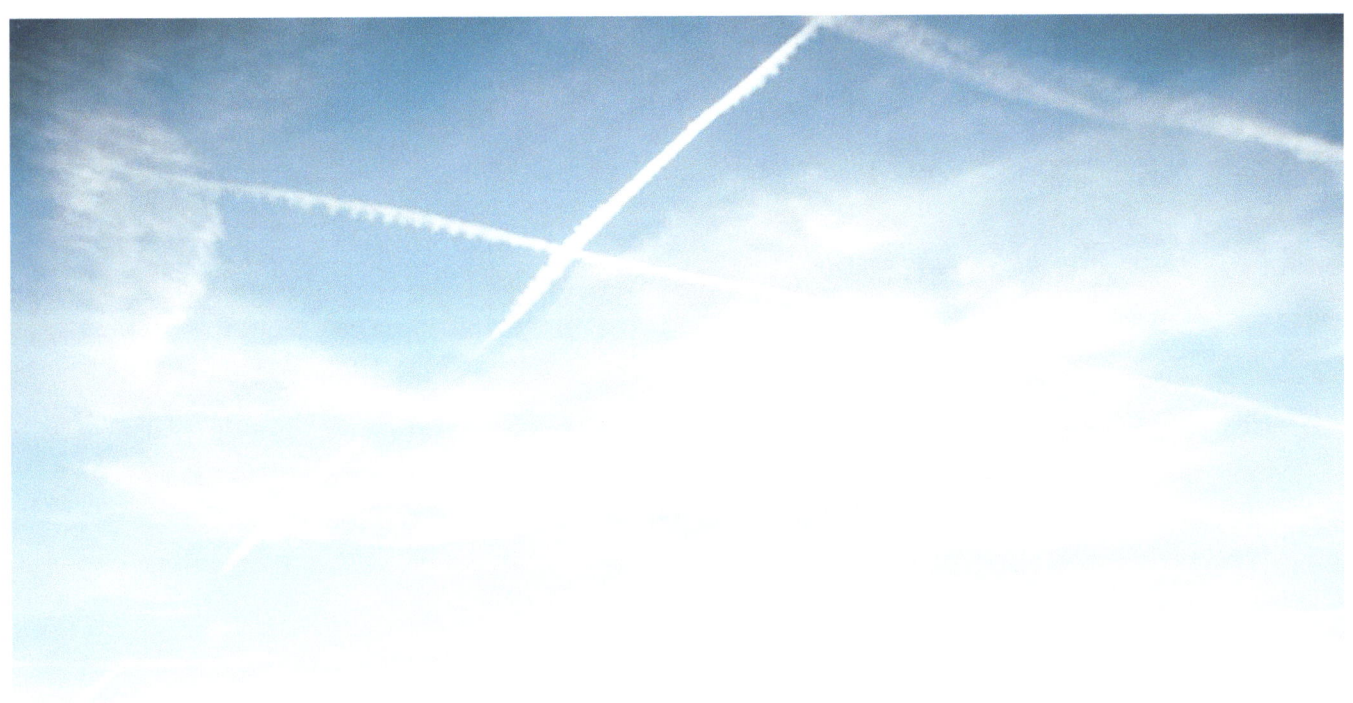

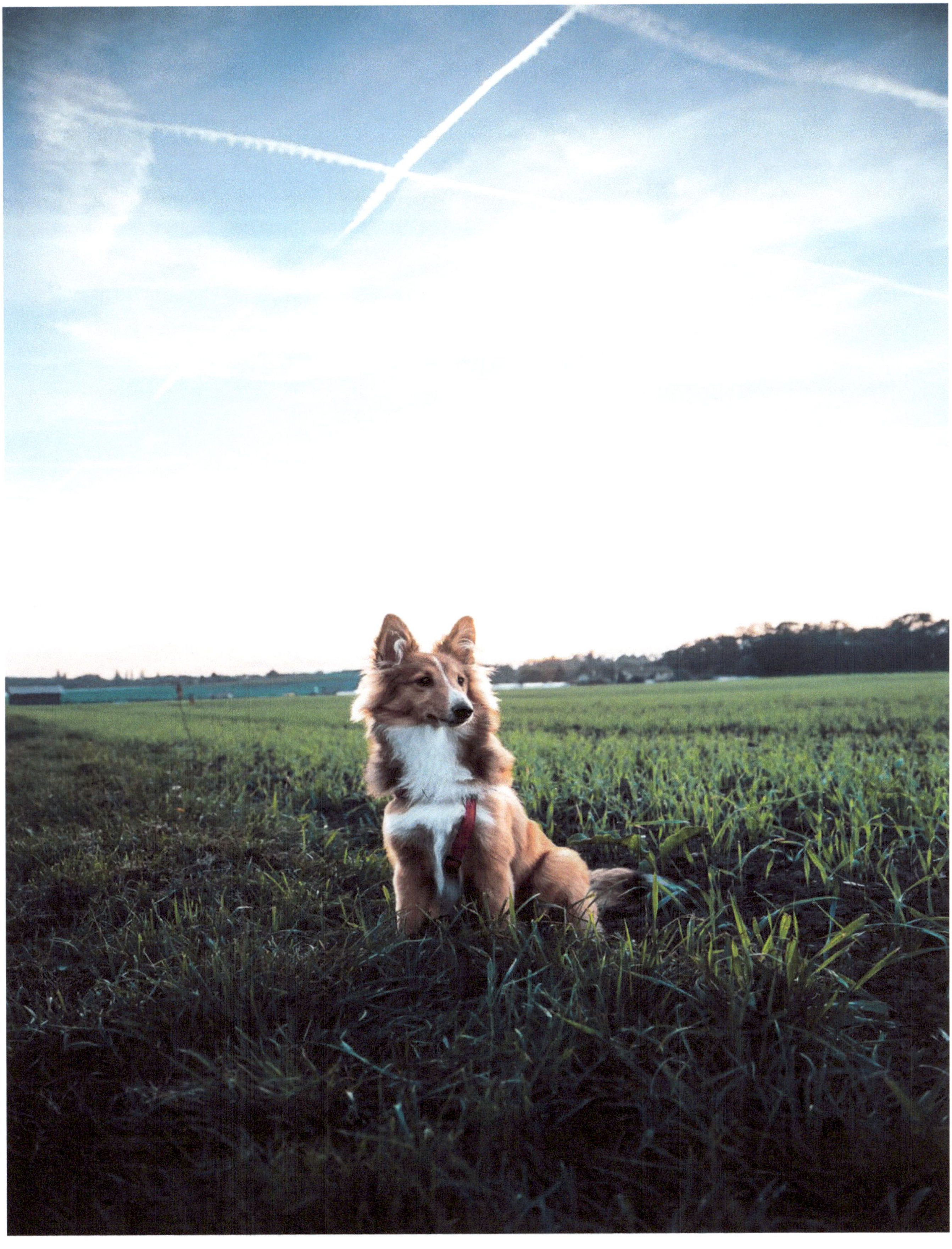

Photographer: Ryan Klaus – Geneva, Switzerland

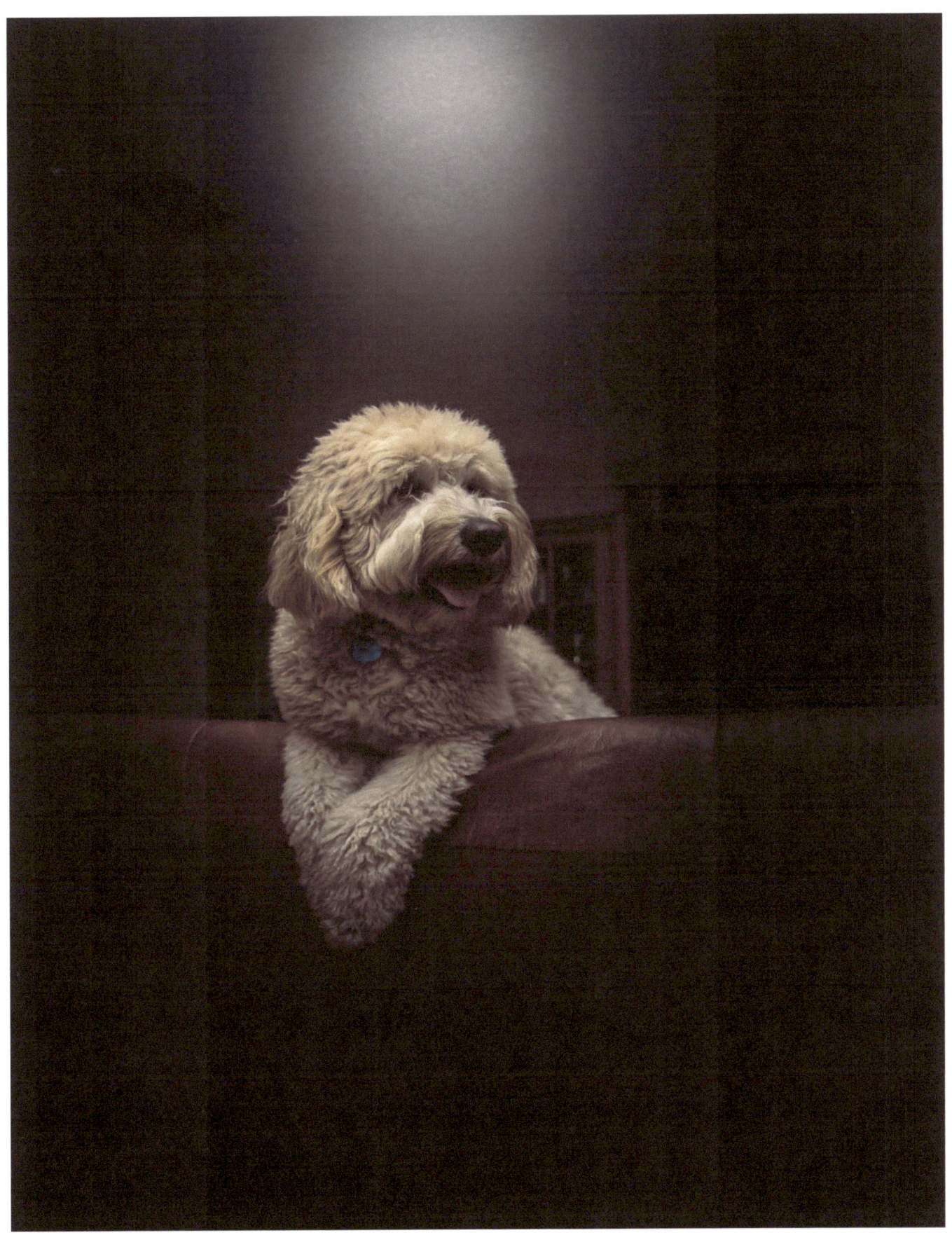

Photographer: Seye Kuyinu

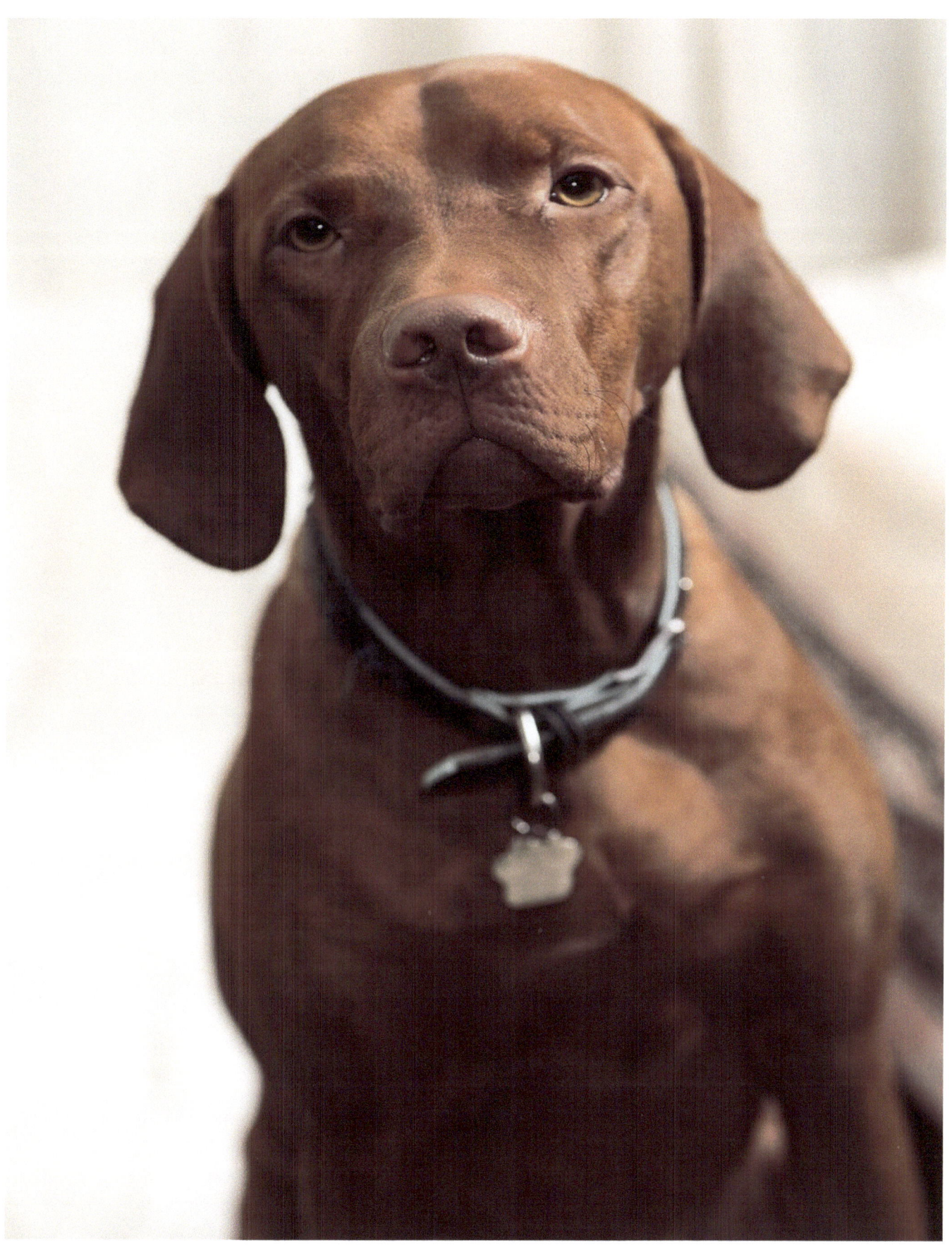

Photographer: Stephen Goldberg

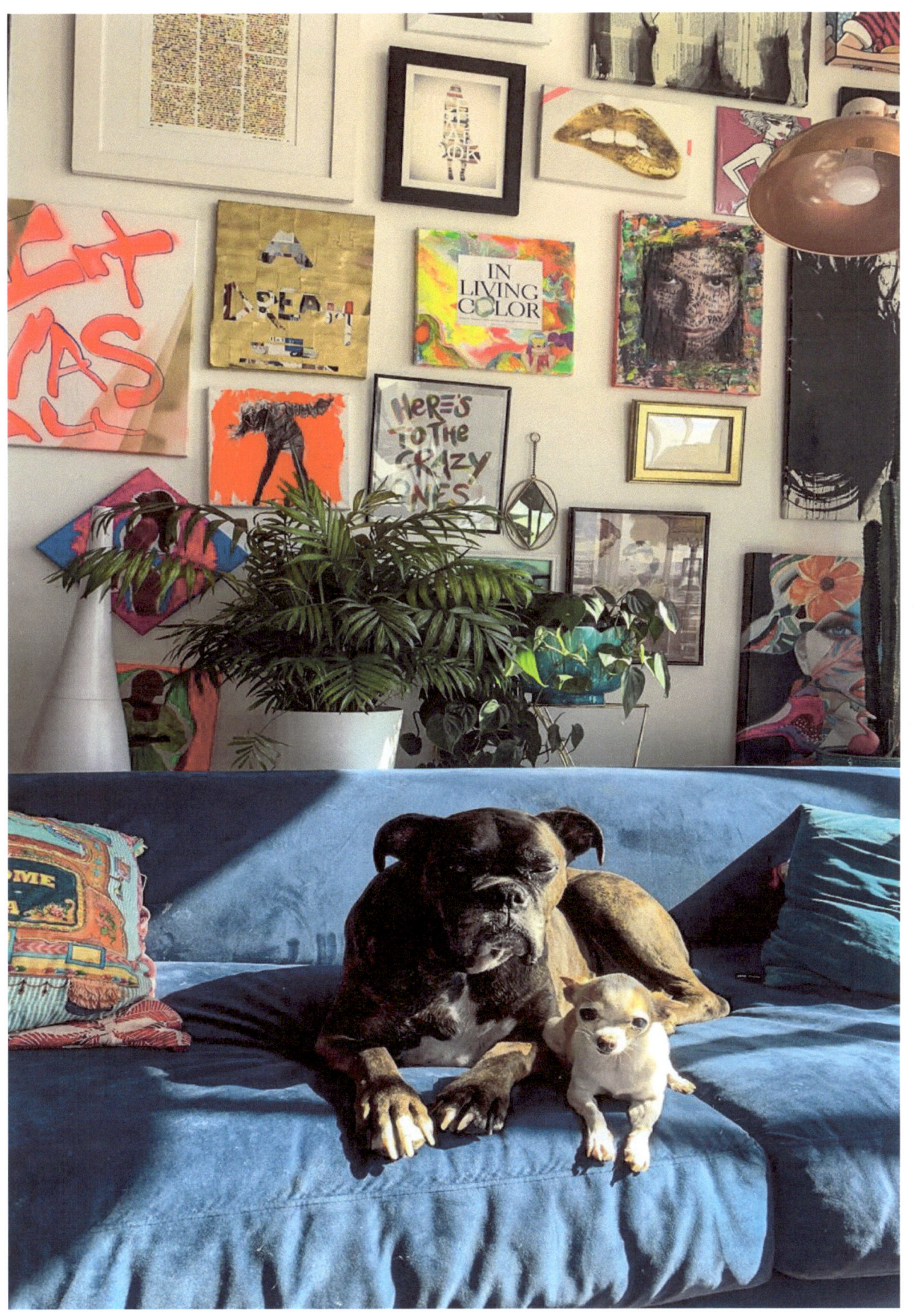

Photographer: Steph Wilson – Denver, CO

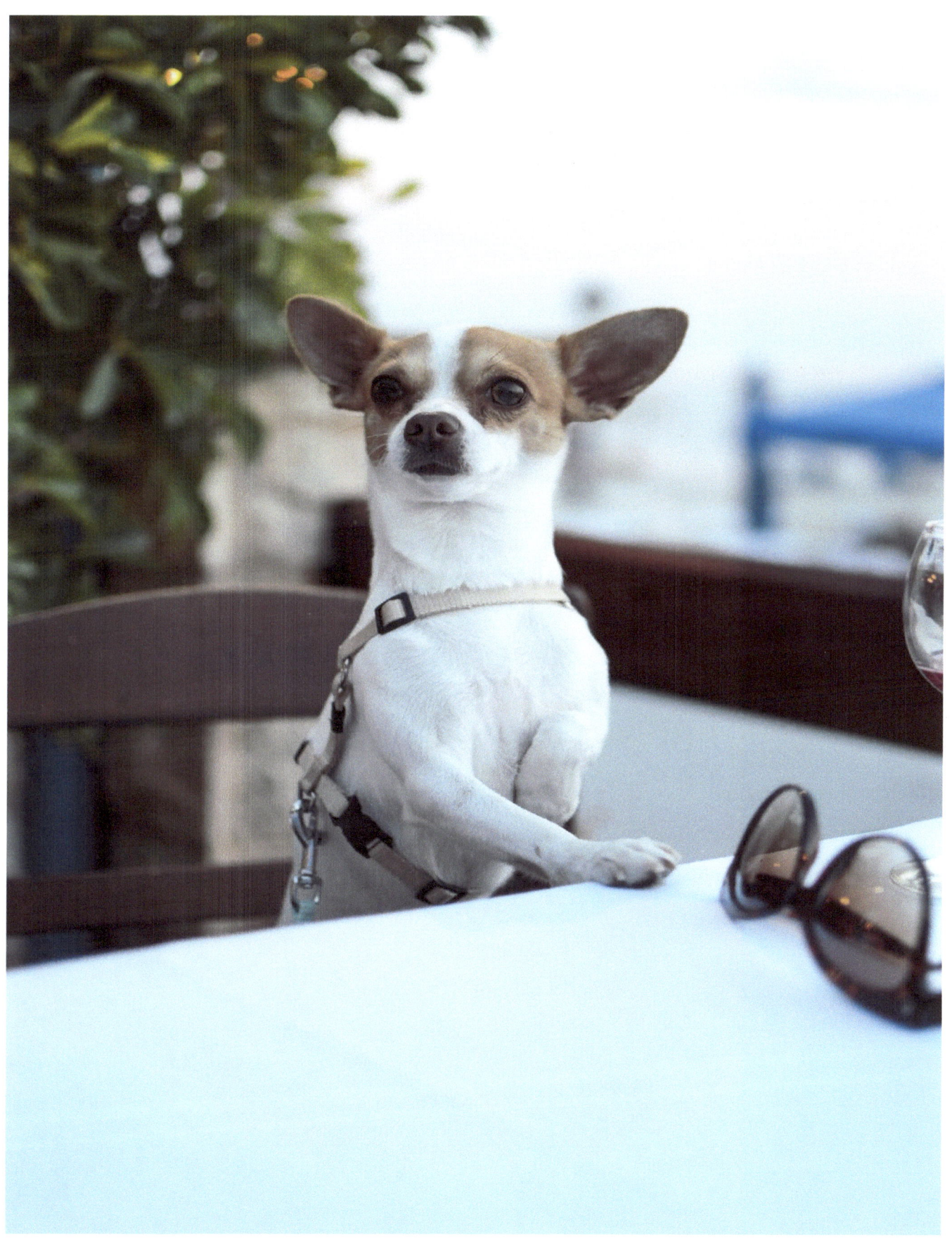

Photographer: Tamara Bellis – Corfu Island, Greece

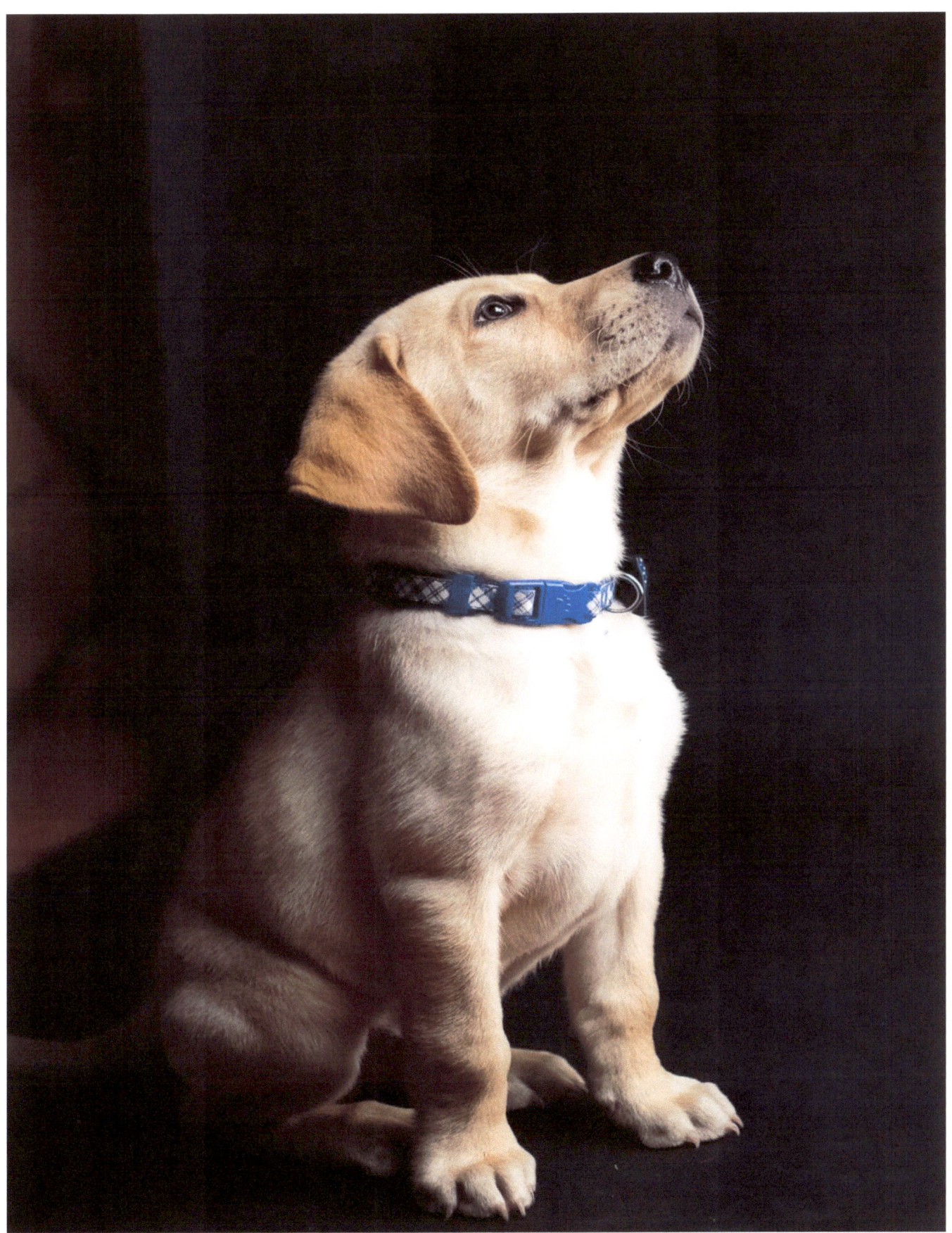

Photographer: Taylor Kopel

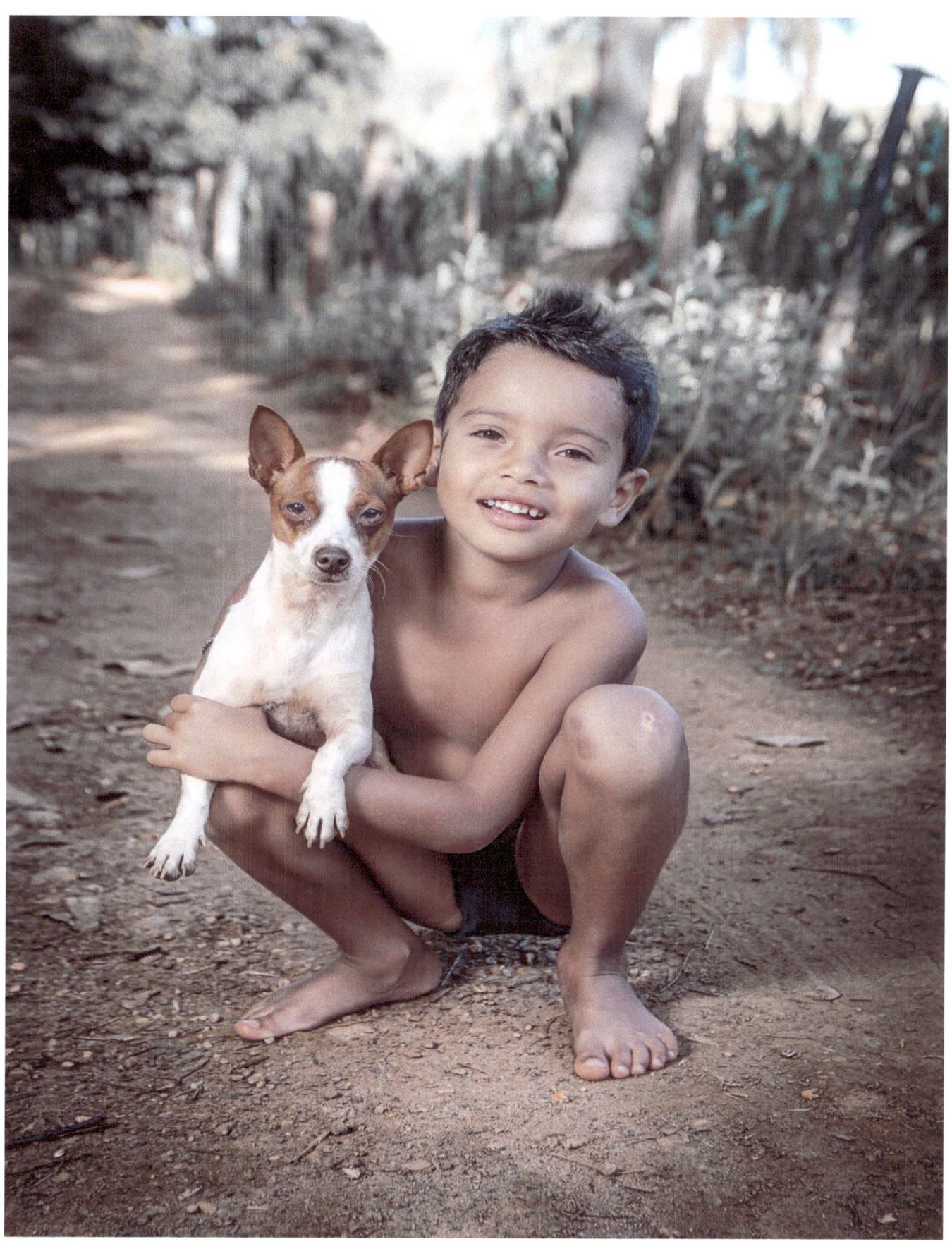

Photographer: Ton Nettos - Brasil

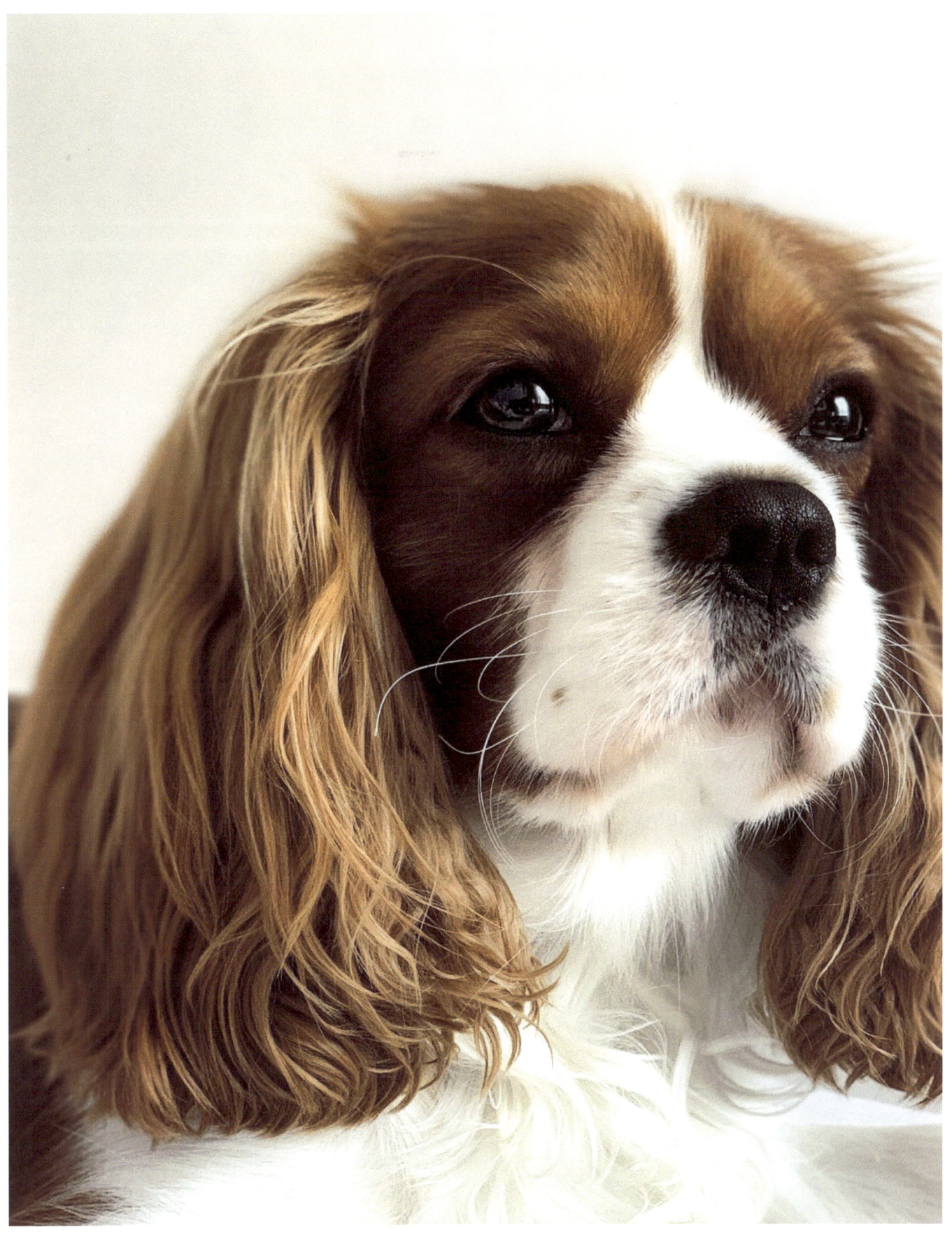

Photographer: T-R Photography - Hungary

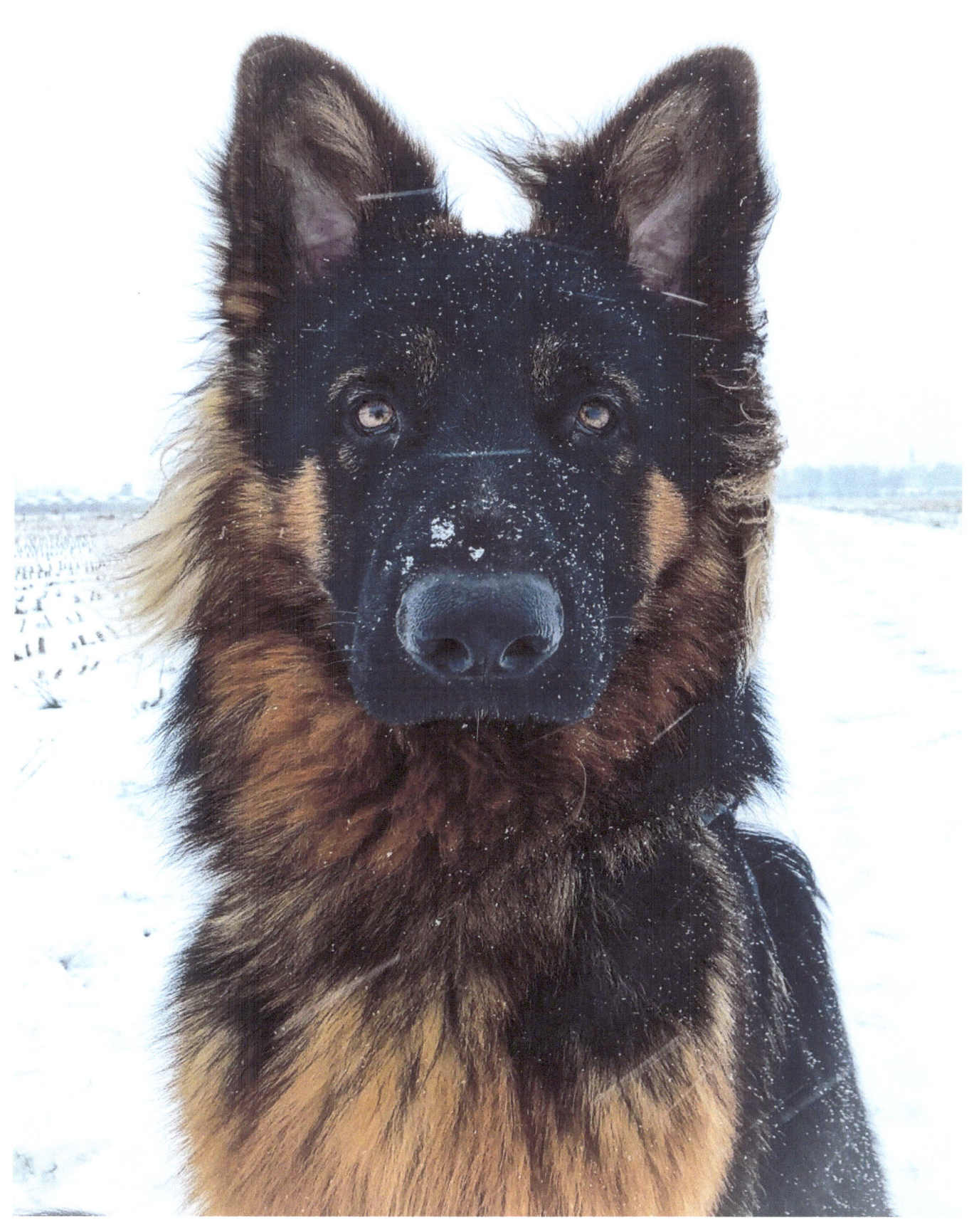

Photographer: Wannes de Mol - Belgium

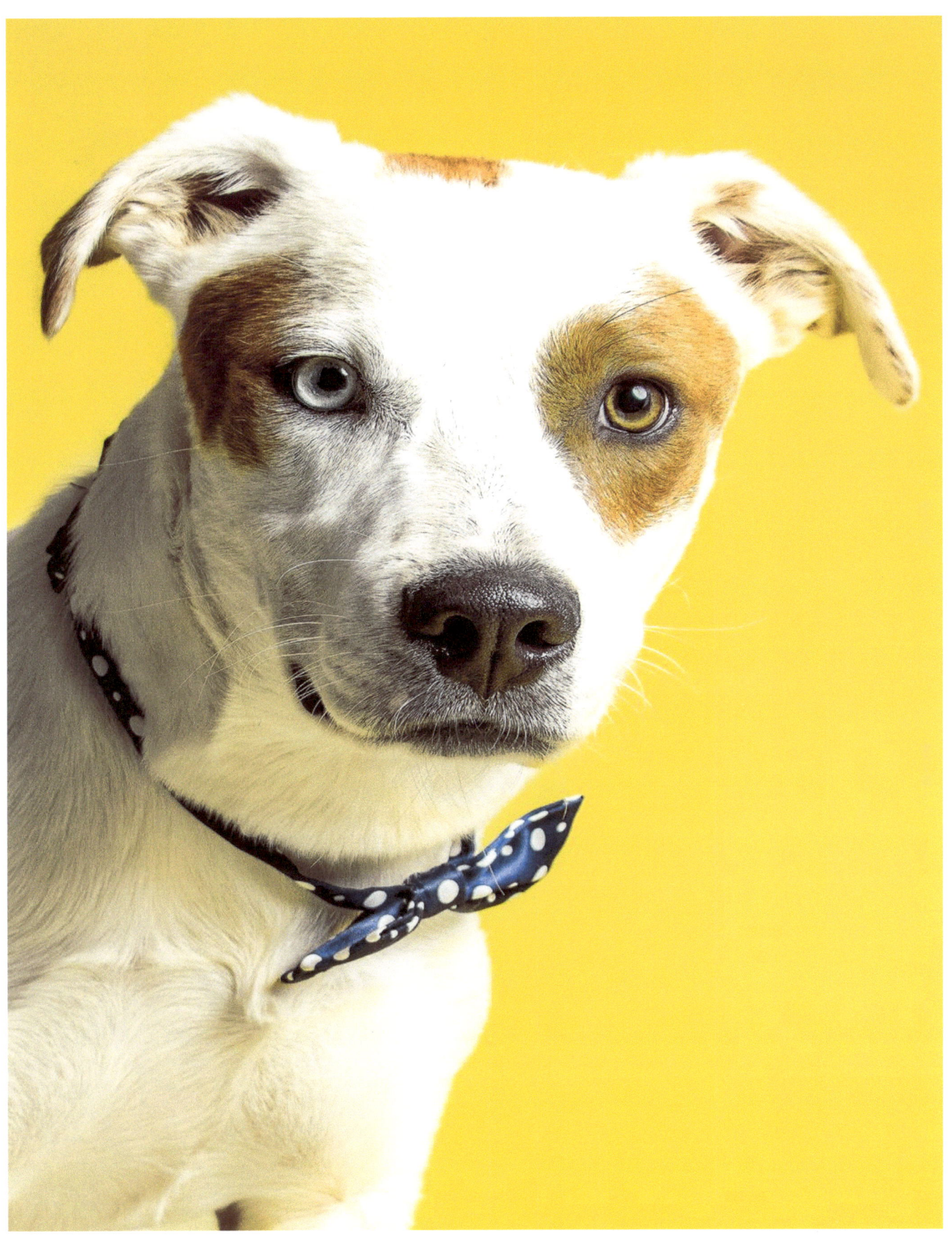

Photographer: Micheal G – New Mexico (Rescue Photographer)